SpringerWienNewYork

Stefan Sonvilla-Weiss

(IN)VISIBLE
Learning to Act in the Metaverse

SpringerWienNewYork

Professor Dr. Stefan Sonvilla-Weiss
ePedagogy Design – Visual Knowledge Building
University of Art and Design Helsinki, TAIK

Printed by support of the Austrian Federal Ministry of Science and Research Vienna

Cover illustration: Stefan Sonvilla-Weiss

SPIN: 12209118
Library of Congress Control Number: 2008928443

With 19 figure pages

ISBN 978-3-211-78538-6 SpringerWienNewYork

Printed in Austria
SpringerWienNewYork is a part of
Springer Science + Business Media
springer.at

Printing and binding: Holzhausen Druck & Medien GmbH,
1140 Wien, Austria

Printed on acid-free and chlorine-free bleached paper

You cannot book in the past

Contents

Acknowledgments

I am especially thankful for the great opportunity I received in parallel with my professor appointment in 2003 at the University of Art and Design Helsinki, TAIK, to develop and steer the international MA program ePedagogy Design – Visual Knowledge Building in cooperation with University Hamburg and Inholland. Several of my topics of concern stress cross-disciplinary thinking and cooperation in contemporary visual media culture, communication theory and media pedagogy. This book is thus dedicated to those who have supported my work over the past years and to those near and far who vitally contributed to shaping and crystallizing my ideas and concepts: Yrjö Sotamaa, Martti Raevaara, Juha Varto, Eija Salmi, Lily Diaz, Owen Kelly from Helsinki, FI, Jaap Jansen (Rotterdam, NL), Torsten Meyer (Hamburg, D), Henry Jenkins (Boston, USA), Peter Weibel (Karlsruhe, D), Mel Alexenberg (Petach Tikvah, IL), Gilles Gervais (Brussels, B), John Tiffin (Wellington, NZ), Yasutaka Shimizu (Tokyo, JP), my global student community, co-workers and affiliates.

My deepest gratitude goes to my wife Barbara, my daughter Felicitas and my son Silvius for their great support and true allegiance during our wanderings abroad over the past seven years, first for two years in Brussels, Belgium, and now for the fifth year in Helsinki, Finland.

Admittedly, without the fabulous online dictionary *leo.org*, this work would hardly have seen the light of day. Special thanks goes to Cindy Kohtala who patiently corrected and transferred my Austrian English into an understandable version.

Introduction

How can real and virtual space interactions generate novel forms of communicative, creative and social practices in global connected communities? Is it possible to avoid unleashing the seemingly inevitable dichotomies in humankind constructing and destroying at the same time? My personal interest in further contributing to the complexity of this discussion is to offer some examples of how the dynamic interplay between technology, culture and sciences calls for novel pedagogical forms and strategies that seek to foster student-centered, self-regulated, participatory, interactive, and immersive learning.

This book thereby deals with the complexity of the global data space and its adherent aspects in social, aesthetic and technological contexts.

To this end I discuss some of the prevalent models of participatory media culture, its historical roots and its creative potential for seamless operation in real and virtual environments. I will also highlight some of the core practices of media production, reception and perception with regard to future concepts of designing and augmenting public and individual data collections for the purpose of creating a gigantic database. In this global connected info space where there is no longer any ontological difference between the real and the virtual, novel forms of human-machine interaction will impact tremendously and pervasively on almost all life issues. Intelligent agents, augmented eyewear, and virtual world avatars and habitats are only a few existing examples that signal the forthcoming changes in networked societies.

The ever-increasing possibilities to interact with computer technology can lead to both techno-utopia and dystopia. A society fully wired and connected is prone to control and surveillance, even though civil counterstrike techniques aim for equiveillance, a state of equilibrium, or at least a desire to attain a state of equilibrium, between surveillance and sousveillance. Are these viable models that will protect us from total control? To what extent are we captivated in complicity, and how can we develop alternative strategies and models without pushing the exit button? And do the virtual and the virtue, interpreted as inseparable experiences of the factual and the fictive, allow for another paradigm shift—co-existence seen as a viable future option in order to survive on this planet?

During the last decade we have seen a nearly all-encompassing approach to the digitalization of knowledge and information stored and circulated in private and public domains. Not only has technology improved in its capacity, pace and scope following the periodical 18-month cycles of Moore's Law, but also our abilities to cope with new cultural techniques commonly subsumed under the label 'digital literacy'. After the rise and fall of the new economy, reliant as it was on the false assumption of transferring the factory model of mass production to a completely different concept of an Internet economy, it took some time to learn from past failures. This new model, which is based not on scarcity but on abundance, forms the primary difference between the Internet economy and the real world. Parallel to the spread of the WWW that emerged out of academic networks, cooperation and collaboration, the free software movement and later open source, have become the congruent architecture and driving force of the Internet up to the present.

In the pursuit of the apparatus, from Freud's "prosthesis god" to "the extension of men" (McLuhan) to wearable computers (Steve Mann), single user interaction has shifted into multiple user interaction on various platforms with either time-based (video sharing), image-based (photo sharing), text-based (blogs and wikis) or audio-based (podcasts) focus. The driving force behind this global move towards self-expression, authenticity and community building is rooted equally in human nature's inherent narcissism and the basic desire to belong to a specific group. Both extremes, idiosyncratic exposure and social networking are phenomena that do not constitute media culture per se, but rather belong to a newly observed phenomenon in current Web 2.0 developments.

Accordingly, two main characteristics drive social media. One dates back to Mark Granovetter's ground-breaking article "The strength of the weak ties" from 1973. Based on a study of job seekers, he discovered that finding a new position does not come through the strong ties (friends or relatives), but through the extended network of weak ties (in over 80% of cases). Similar observations can be made inside "social utility tools" (Facebook) that connect people with friends and others who work, study and live around them. This so-called long tail effect also has implications for the producers of content, especially those whose products could not—for economic reasons —find a place in pre-Internet information distribution channels controlled by book publishers, record companies, movie studios, and television networks. From the producers' standpoint, the Long Tail has made possible a flowering of creativity across all fields of human endeavor. One example of this surge is YouTube, where thousands of diverse videos—whose content, production value or lack of popularity make them inappropriate for traditional television—are easily accessible to a wide range of viewers.

It is exactly this spirit of participation, cooperation and sharing that has fundamentally changed media perception, reception and production. The shift from implicit (tacit knowledge) to explicit forms of knowledge sharing has paved the way for new forms of collective intelligence, which one pioneer, George Pór, defined as "the capacity of human communities to evolve towards higher order complexity and harmony, through such innovation mechanisms as differentiation and integration, competition and collaboration."(http://www.community-intelligence.com/blogs/public/)

As the entire media architecture has shifted from pure consumerism to a creative participatory media culture, the user is no longer reliant on a single expert opinion. Instead, he can refer to multiple and multimodal information resources to be validated, structured and organized through peer review and intelligent agents. Consequently the enormous amount of information and knowledge resources available on ubiquitous, circumfluent displays in private and public spaces raises new questions on private/public safety, control, and legal issues, for example in consumer detection. "You can't hide anything anymore," says Don Tapscott, co-author of *The Naked Corporation*, a book about corporate transparency, and *Wikinomics*. Thus the core truth is this: If you are in the web, people will find out.

Yet what becomes visible to ordinary Web users displays only a small fraction (15%) of the much bigger, invisible deep Web, content that is not part of the surface Web indexed by search engines.

The "world" is turned "outside in" (the physical is being represented in the virtual), and the metaverse is going "inside out" (virtually-controlled sensors are permeating the physical world). Will it be possible in the future to express our thoughts, feelings, emotions and desires through an electronic communication system?

In this context, the observation tools of an Augmented

Reality world are turned inward, serving as an adjunct memory. Lifelogging systems are used to capture both the practical and the transient. Besides the political implications, they also have significant personal implications: do we envisage a world knowing that everything we say or do is likely to be recorded? Is the answer a concept of radical transparency and authenticity, or do we simply wish to become invisible, undetected—a blank sheet, an empty record in the data-space?

"Trust" is not a viable concept either, at least for those concerned about liberal democracy, social justice and the welfare state. It is a morally ambiguous concept that can easily turn into anti-utopia. Terrorist attacks and their aftermath have shown us how drastic the effects were on widely divergent levels of control over and access to information, especially personal information.

Open source principles such as radical transparency, meritocracy, consensus, and networked collaboration that were discarded long ago by business are nowadays the greatest word-of-mouth amplifier in history: consumers learn to trust peers more and companies less. A similar trend is true for businesses and institutions that are shifting from command and control to processes of sharing observations, concerns and suggestions with the intention of improving the customer/client relationship. At the same time every transaction an individual makes on the Internet leaves behind a traceable consumer profile that can be turned into profitable business. Thus, coming back to the techniques of sousveillance, it appears paradoxical to solve a problem with the same means that actually caused the problem. The assumption of reciprocity-based control in networking culture, which is driven by power laws, conflicts with the hegemonic claims of global capitalism. The mechanisms of control are in fact a non-zero-sum game.

Somewhat metaphorically though, I introduce the concept of camouflage as a tactic of survival, ranging from concealing species in nature to traditional pattern paintings, radar-absorbing dark paint, liquid crystal displays up to phased array optics applying a three-dimensional hologram of background scenery. I will also argue that the human quest for the perfect cloaking device repeats the mythology of Perseus, who went equipped with a helm of invisibility to kill Medusa. This kind of synopsis, the combination of two "realities" by means of human vision and a technical apparatus, together with the magic helm of invisibility, makes Perseus a prototypical example of today's advanced technology-supported warfare tactics. Nevertheless, technologies increasingly reliant on vision surveillance systems suggest a need for strike-back strategies that are neither individual, nor vision-based. As visual information increasingly becomes digital data fed into distributed databases, any kind of inverse surveillance technique must therefore implicate data manipulation and obliteration.

Spanning the spectrum of interrelated artistic questions and scientific findings, the reader will gain new insights from the standpoint of the "Phenomenology of Perception" (Merleau-Ponty, 1945) and cognitive neuroscience: as the body is the basis for our interactions and perceptions, virtual space can only be seen as a symbiotic synthesis of technology and corporeal phenomena. Consequently, the construction of self in virtual environments follows an alternative mode of "representation", which synergizes the physical and the virtual: the mind and body become one in order to pursue a unified goal.

This experience of virtual reality illusions reflects Baudrillard's wishful thinking—yet in other contexts—to return back to appearance in the world of illusions rather than disappearing in the world of simulations. When there is no more real, the frontiers blur between facts and information, between information and entertainment, between entertainment and politics. The result is an overarching aesthetization of everything; thus, contemporary art has become interchangeable, based on its self-referential autonomy.

Concepts of remediation that oscillate between artistic strategies, techniques and concepts are however in a constant flux of imaginary and representative approximation upon an initial concept, an idea that undergoes several processes until it reaches a certain kind of permutation, regardless of whether it is reality or fiction, fact or fantasy, authenticity or simulation.

Navigation, orientation and communication in real and virtual surroundings become increasingly context dependent in ambient intelligent environments. Will this lead to a union of human and machine, combining the knowledge and skills embedded in our brains with the vastly greater capacity, speed, and knowledge-sharing ability of our own creative manifestations?

Or will this mean a radical suspension or demise of our innate sensual abilities in the future? A rather different approach that brings us back to human evolution relates to the concept of Consciousness Singularity: the idea that it is impossible for us to imagine "what it's like" with our current limited cognitive abilities. Our brain is deceptive in terms of visual perception and interpretation, and the link between what we expect to see, and what our brain tells us we actually see, is an imaginative one.

The final chapter deals with some of the most prevalent questions relating to proximities of scientific and artistic engagement in light of educational change. I will argue that paradigmatic changes in the process of renewing and preserving the conditions of cultural self-organization are key to a major shift in how we construct knowledge, technology and cultural memory.

However, novel theoretical delineations of model, game and communication knowledge in different contexts have had less impact on learning and knowledge organization thus far. The audiovisual restructuring of knowledge and communication in interrelated and cooperating fields extended by neurophysiological research into cognition and perception will affect institutions and the individual, resulting in a conceptual lag in both teachings and research.

Not only are knowledge and media technology changing rapidly, but learning attitudes and styles are also changing fluidly across different technologies, interfaces and modes of interaction.

Learning to act in the metaverse is a plea, a suggestion and an invitation to the reader to continue with this discussion.

1 Global Data Space: Early Visionaries

With the advent of telematic culture at the end of the 19th century, a new consciousness arose out of the many inventions made to shorten both mental and physical distances in "local thinking and global acting" (Buckminster Fuller).

Otto Neurath (1882-1944) and Paul Otlet (1868-1944) were only a few of the visionaries who reached out to explore novel ways of organizing, visualizing and disseminating knowledge on a global level. Taking into account each of the scholar's uniqueness, the unifying umbrella under which their scientific contribution might be subsumed is the spirit of universal modernity in order to promote the progress of science, social welfare, and new international institutions. Their work necessarily both contributed to and reflected strong intellectual and social concerns of the times, a period characterized by the increasingly complex and dynamic movement for the international organization of scientific relations and the international regulation of what we now call communications. It was shaped by the crisis of the First World War and the transformative after-effects of that catastrophic event.

Some of the key problems were how fundamental units of information were to be identified, encoded in various ways, represented visually, and deployed educationally and in various planning contexts so that social progress might be accelerated. Possible solutions that were explored involved attempts to design new linguistic formations ranging from standardized systems of signs and procedures for various professional architectural and urban planning tasks (e.g. Le Corbusier) to artificial international and auxiliary languages. Some of the figures involved with aspects of these issues struggled to find a "world view" that would underpin the creation of new kinds of international organizations and that would eventually guide both national programs of social change and the formation of a new world policy.

Issues of internationalization, globalization, transformation and the architecture of knowledge were already being investigated at that time, with specific emphasis on redefining the roles, practices and organizational arrangements of libraries and museums in collecting, disseminating, cumulating, and displaying informative artifacts; creating worldwide "documentary" networks; and developing collaboratively centralized depositories of scientific data.

Both Otlet and Neurath were committed in their different ways to a pervasive modernist belief in rationality, planning, standardization, the value of the scientific method and the inevitability of scientific and social progress as they conceptualized and attempted to solve "information" problems.

Paul Otlet: Information Architect

At the end of the nineteenth century, Paul Otlet (1868-1944), for many years a central figure in the development of information science, anticipated modern ideas about hypertext. Otlet demonstrated a "monographic principle" according to which text should be broken down into its intellectually important constituent parts, which should then be separately recorded. The application of this principle produced what in hypertext terms would be called nodes. These nodes were to be linked for flexible searching by the Universal Decimal Classification (Fig. 1), the first of the great faceted (or synthetic) classification schemes, developed by Otlet and his colleagues.

In 1910, consequent to the Brussels World's Fair, the two Belgian lawyers Otlet and LaFontaine started their project as the centerpiece of a new 'world city'—a huge archive containing collections such as the International Museum, the International Library, the International Bibliographic Catalog and the Universal Documentary Archives. These collections were to be conceived as parts of one universal body of documentation: in essence, an encyclopedic survey of human knowledge, as an enormous intellectual warehouse of books, documents, catalogs and scientific objects. The collection grew to a gigantic archive of 12 million index cards and documents.[1]

Otlet was specifically interested in what he called the "synthetical movement", in which he explored the educational perspectives of an International Museum center within the Mundaneum. Modern education should accord with his notions of "universalist synthesis".[2] He expressed his underlying premise in the slogan: "for universal civilization, universalist education" (ibid.: 10). For this kind of synthesis-oriented education he proposed great emphasis needed to be placed on teaching media. He believed that there should be "didactic charts and tables" which displayed diagrammatically, schematically and therefore in a simplified form the most essential knowledge. Moreover, he was convinced of the value of film in teaching: "Visualization on the screen will become a fundamental teaching method," he declared (ibid.: 3).

At the Museum Center a 'finding list' would be established of important educational materials, and Otlet, who was fully aware of the problematic implications of preparing and distributing useful abstracts, expressed his appreciation of the potential value for education of recent technological developments such as

> *Mechanical instruments:*
> these instruments will have a great future in teaching. They are automatic auxiliaries to the teacher, the extension of the word and the book. Without a doubt, they are a long way from being perfect, but what marvelous progress has already been made. The gramophone has assisted the teaching of language greatly… It can do some for the music. The Pianola will permit the acquisition of an extensive knowledge of music, of works which one should hear. Machines for projecting fixed dispositive plates or microfilms (photoscope), the cinema in black and white and in colour, with texts interspersed in the film with the possibility of interrupting it, will allow knowledge of things and actions which should be seen.
> The radio with its personal apparatus and its great speakers, its musical programs, its lectures, its courses, will permit one to be in direct contact with the outside world, to receive messages, to observe the usefulness of foreign languages, to attempt to understand them.
> *New Teaching Equipment:*
> education based on the considerations developed here will necessitate the development of teaching materials. The poor material which educational establishments use today, will no longer be satisfactory. (ibid.: 24)

Otlet envisaged the production of new forms of textbooks through international cooperation, and with all the new materials and methods gathered from around the world, he believed that teaching establishments would become a "little world", a kind of a microcosm for

> infants at the primary level, colleges, lycées for young people at the secondary level. Static objects, functioning objects, materials to be observed, experimented with, used for a workshop, the school museum. In the form of manuals and publications this material should be the result of collective work, of a continuous collaboration involving teachers of all countries, of all levels, and of every educational speciality. (ibid.: 25)

Otlet's vision of access to the "world-archive" by people from the comfort of their own homes has met its best realization in the invention of the WWW up to the participatory approach of Wikipedia. In Otlet's last book, *Monde* (1935), he articulated a final vision of the great "réseau"[3] that may as well serve as his last word:

> Everything in the universe, and everything of man, would be registered at a distance as it was produced. In this way a moving image of the world will be established, a true mirror of his memory. From a distance, everyone will be able to read text, enlarged and limited to the desired subject, projected on an individual screen. In this way, everyone from his armchair will be able to contemplate creation, as a whole or in certain of its parts. (Otlet, 390-391)

Given this statement, Otlet believed that documents could best be understood in a dynamic system taking into account their relationship to place, time, language, other readers, writers and topics—to highlight the social dimension. Otlet attached very much importance to the empirical truth ("fac-

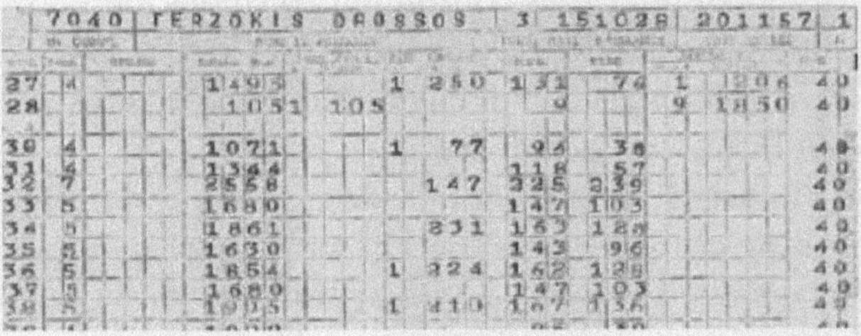

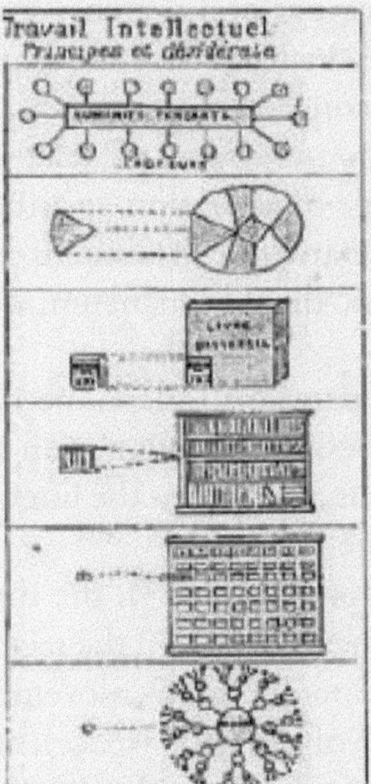

Universal Decimal Classification (UDC)
= A document may be classified under a combination of different categories through the use of additional symbols.

+ (plus)
Addition, e.g. 59+636 = Zoology and animal breeding

/ (stroke)
Extension, e.g. 592/599 = Systematic zoology
(everything from 592 to 599 inclusive)

: (colon)
Relation, e.g. 17:7 Relation of ethics to art

1 Classification scheme, machine nodes and search functions

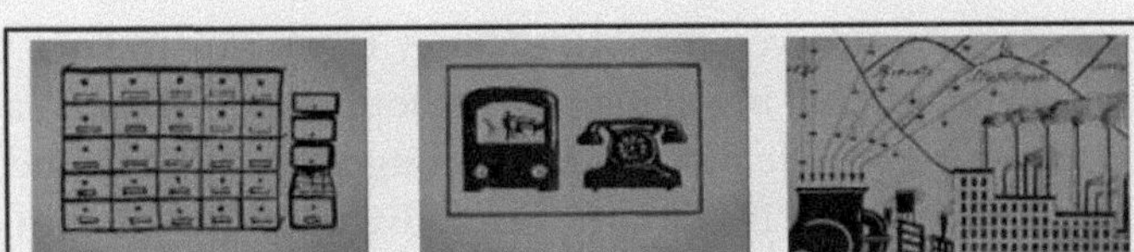

ticity") being considered as continuing collaboration between readers and writers. Hence, the imprint ("trail") each user would leave on a single document would then become part of the explicit history of each document.

Otlet envisaged the idea of a "living encyclopedia" illuminated both by objective classification and by the direct influence of readers and writers: a system simultaneously ordered and self-organizing, and endlessly re-configurable by the individual reader or writer. He used drawings and sketches quite experimentally to make visible his fascinating ideas about globalization and universalism. In his concept drawing (Fig. 2) "le réseau mondial," Otlet depicts the processes and relationships of the institutions for knowledge organization creating a network that leads the citizen in a hierarchical structure to the great central knowledge organization, the Mundaneum, as a physical institution.

If we look at the communication means, telephone and screen, Otlet conceived as an ideal desktop configuration for scholars, it becomes obvious that he has anticipated the interactive and hypermedial dimension of the Internet.

In this visualization of Le Plan Mondial (Fig. 3), the three visible sides of the cube represent 1) the domains, 2) the sectors and 3) the instruments of the world plan. The cube's movement along the three axes labelled 4 (degree of reach), 5 (space), and 6 (time), would change the relationships between the data.[4]

The vision of interconnected media Otlet outlined in his "Encyclopedia Universalis Mundane"[5] resembles today's teleconferencing setup involving the gramophone, film, radio and television (Fig.4). He imagined an arrangement of multimedia machines having an important interactive capability that in effect could create a virtual space.

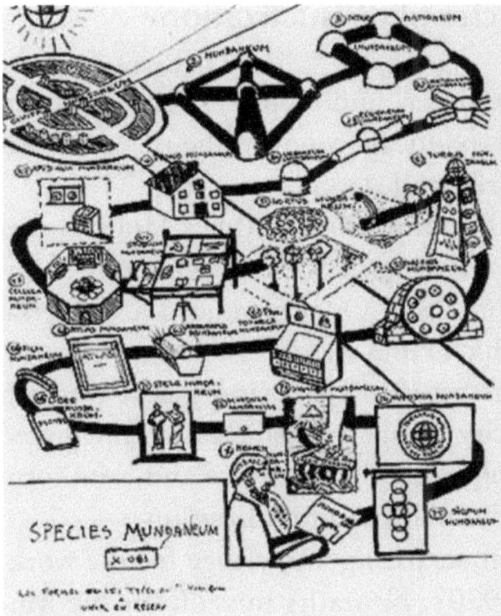

2 The future city of knowledge as envisioned by Otlet

On peut figurer ces six ordres de données par un cube aux trois dimension (1,2,3) et mobile suivant trois grands axes (4,5,6).

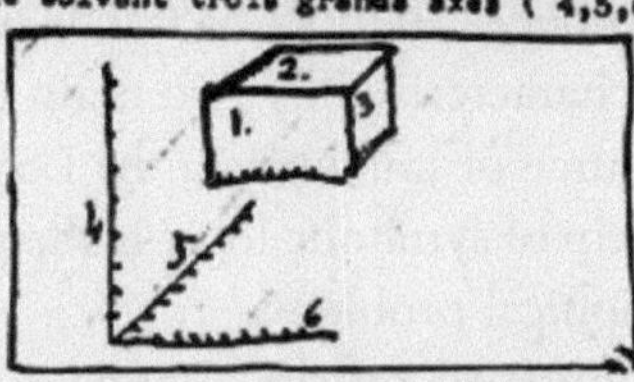

3 Spatial information organization system

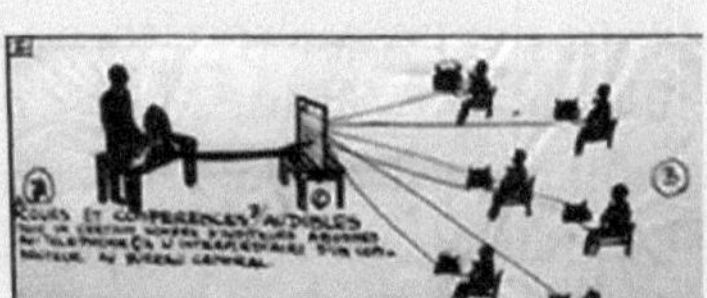

4 The first interconnected multimedia machines envisioned by Otlet

Otto Neurath: Socioscientific Visualization

Otto Neurath (1882-1945) was undoubtedly a revolutionary thinker in socialist policy, political economy, the theory of science, sociology and in social philosophy.

It was Paul Otlet and his foundation of Palais Mondial that became vital to Neurath's development of the Museum of Society and Economy in Vienna. If Otlet envisaged a Universal approach to culture in which cities were worlds in microcosm, collapsing the distinction between space and place, Neurath conversely imagined a city in macrocosm, as an integrated community with a consolidated infrastructure and a uniform system of governance and economic administration.

In his approach to democratizing knowledge for the working class people in the 1920's, Neurath's mission for the Museum of Society and Economy therefore sought to make comprehensible rational thinking and engender social transparency. Neurath was a member of the Vienna Circle, whose philosophical direction was characterized by two main beliefs: a) Experience is the only source of knowledge; b) Logical analysis performed with the help of symbolic logic is the preferred method for solving philosophical problems.[6]

The final goal pursued by the Vienna Circle was unified science, that is, the construction of a "constitutive system" in which every legitimate statement is reduced to the concepts of lower level which refer directly to the given experience. The Vienna Circle was especially influenced by Ernst Mach's philosophy of Science, which also influenced the logical positivism of the early 20th century. Mach held that accepting objective reality being composed of sensations and not of material things would make the subject of psychology and physics indistinguishable. Hence the difference between the two scientific disciplines is not related to the subject but merely how we approach it.

> The unity of consciousness is not an argument in point. Since the apparent antithesis between the real world and the world given through the senses lies entirely in our mode of view, and no actual gulf exists between them, a complicated and variously interconnected content of consciousness is no more difficult to understand than is the complicated interconnection of the world.
> If we regard the ego as a real unity, we become involved in the following dilemma: either we must set over against the ego a world of unknowable entities (which would be quite idle and purposeless), or we must regard the whole world, the egos of other people included, as comprised in our own ego (a proposition to which it is difficult to yield serious assent).
> But if we take the ego simply as a practical unity, put together for purposes of provisional survey, or as a more strongly cohering group of elements, less strongly connected with other groups of this kind, questions like those above discussed will not arise, and research will have an unobstructed future. [7]

The persistence of metaphysics in the manifesto of the Viennese Circle is connected not only with the ambiguity of natural language but also with "social and economic struggles". Metaphysics and theology are allied to traditional social forms, while the group of people who "faces modern times, rejects these views and takes its stand on the ground of empirical sciences" (cf. Nozick, 339).

Thus the struggle between metaphysics and scientific world

conception is not only a struggle between different kinds of philosophies, but it is also—and perhaps primarily—a struggle between different political, social and economic attitudes. Neurath, who was left wing, consequently interpreted the scientific world conception as an approach towards education, upbringing, architecture, and the shaping of economic and social life.

The most unique thing about the Museum of Society and Economy was that it encompassed Vienna's nascent mass culture. Neurath believed that common forms of entertainment such as popular films or cartoons offered museum curators and educators a new and highly powerful platform through which to dispense scientific information: "Modern man receives a large part of his knowledge through pictorial impressions," he observed, "illustrations, lantern slides, films. The daily newspaper disseminates more and more pictures every day. With that comes also advertising, which on the one hand works with optical signals and on the other hand also with representations. Exhibitions, museums are thoroughly products of this drive to watch."[8]

As mass media became more and more powerful by the middle of the 1920's—there were already 560 000 weekly filmgoers in Vienna (one quarter of the city's entire population)—this reality carried major implications for the nature and culture of communication. Neurath was acutely aware that mass forms of communication were superior because they could reach broader audiences and required less concentration and energy. He observed that for average people the most comfortable way to receive education is partly during their period of rest, and through optical impressions. This led Neurath to the conclusion that a) the dissemination of socio-scientific education requires similar means of representation as modern advertise-

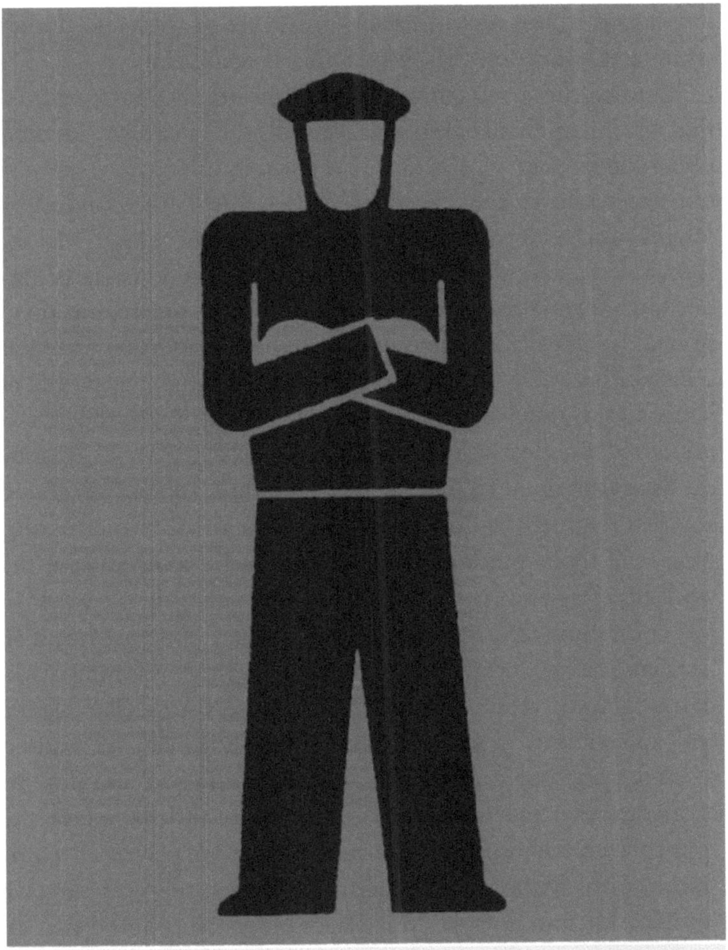

5 ISOTYPE pictogram, International Picture Language

ments and b) the dissemination of images or pictures (Bilder) stimulates education (Bildung) and self-realization.

During the arrangement of exhibitions, Neurath realized that the most challenging part would be to visualize *invisible* phenomena, that is, social and economic processes that were not accessible to the naked eye. Therefore he responded by establishing a department of transformation, which was responsible for distilling scientific facts down to clusters of important information and developing ways of organizing them in a pedagogically effective manner. The 'transformer' acted as a liaison between the scientific community and the public at large, and its task was to organize the information so that it was presented as effectively as possible. The collection of statistical data attempted to provide for the public a more integrated and less fragmented understanding of the modern metropolis. Neurath's main intention was to familiarize and educate the working class about the broader systems of order at work in the contemporary city—not just its visual systems, but also its quantitative, social and political ones. By developing a system of graphic representation that made statistical data legible and accessible to non-specialized mass audiences, he wanted to bridge the gap between reading and seeing in an effort to accelerate the transmission of information and to reduce the role that convention, custom and education played in communication. Exploring the contrast between how we perceive information and how we create knowledge, he believed that an iconic system could stimulate the intellect and imagination in a way that scripture could not.

> A man coming into a strange country without a knowledge of the language is uncertain where to get his ticket at the station

> or the harbor, where to put his boxes, how to make use of the telephone in the telephone box, where to go in the post office. But if he sees pictures by the side of the strange words, they will put him on the right path.[9]

His approach to communication theory was particularly remarkable, by investigating the role of visual communication in early modernism.

From today's perspective, however, it remains ambiguous to consider Neurath's thinking, especially if we look at the political circumstances in the 1920's and 1930's and today's reality of electronic media landscape that is in sharp contrast to the "the Age of Mechanical Reproduction" (Benjamin). It seems there is literally nothing left of the socialist utopia of a new society for which Neurath had concrete expectations.

Neurath's efforts to unify science with an all-encompassing clarity in representing scientific results and transfering knowledge to society corresponds with his central credo: to engage science for the wellbeing of society. Neurath's scepticism of rigorous scientific boundaries inevitably connects to Richard Rorty's pragmatism about truth and other matters and to a Wittgensteinian philosophy of language which declares that meaning is a social-linguistic product and sentences do not 'link up' with the world in a direct correspondence.

Together with his intention to develop an universally understandable pictorial language, a broader educational approach with specific emphasis on adult education became an important issue for Neurath.

Scientific argument should thus be made plausible through "an education through the eye" for which Neurath developed pictorial statistics, a visual display of quantitative information

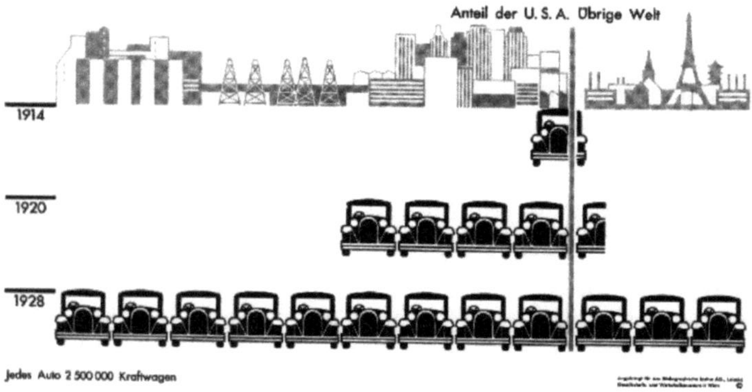

6 Pictorial statistics

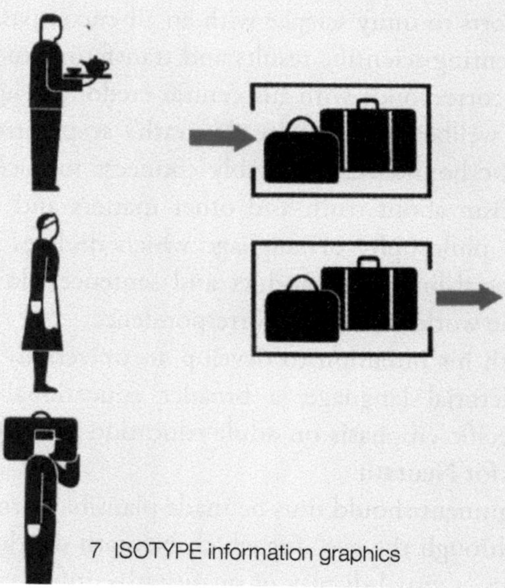

7 ISOTYPE information graphics

that became internationally recognized as ISOTYPE (International System of Picture Education). In Neurath's view systematization of visual representation can be achieved by the objectivity of perceivable visual information (based on findings in Gestalt psychology in the late 19th century) rather than by words or figures (Fig. 5).

In one of his essays (Bildliche Darstellung sozialer Tatbestände, Pictorial Representation of Social Facts), he came to the conclusion that words separate and pictures unite. ("Worte trennen, Bilder verbinden.") In that respect the advent of media technology at the turn of the 19th century did support Neurath's ambitions to reach out to the underprivileged in order to pursue a visual approach to education.

According to his development of the Viennese method of Visual Education, Neurath favored the practical implementation of visual communication, what he called pictorial statistics (Fig. 6).

> A picture produced after the rules of the Viennese Method shows the most important details of the object at first glance; apparent differences must strike the eye immediately. At second glance, it should be possible to distinguish the more important details, and at third glance, whatever other details to be seen. If a picture gives further information at fourth or at fifth glance, it should be rejected as pedagogically unsuitable according to the Viennese School.[10]

Neurath's method referred to a set of newly created visual signs whose relation to an object should bear the highest possible iconicity. With this sign system consistency (the same signs for the same things), and scalability (proportion/quantity relationship) were as important as the transferability and variability of the sign system for different educational purposes. ISOTYPE thus became the visual code of picturing knowledge (Fig. 7).

This program was to introduce media literacy as promoting a new form of enlightenment, replacing argumentative-linear decoding as the exclusive form of the scientific argument with new forms of iconic communication and consistent visualization:

> Visual impressions have become more and more important in our "visual era," and especially to unschooled adults and to children. The usual visual methods – even the most careful charts and the most elaborate exhibits – are frequently confusing rather than enlightening, because their elements are unfamiliar.
> It is almost as though people had to learn a new language for each new communication.
> One solution is ISOTYPE, a method with a special visual dictionary and a special visual grammar; that is, a new visual world, comparable to our book and word world.
> Charts, pictures, models, movies, games, illustrations can, with a little related text, show in this symbol language the main facts and explain the important problems in any field of knowledge.
> The basic aim of this visual method is to humanize and democratize the world of knowledge and of intellectual activity.
> The best foundation for a comprehensive visual education would be to let all children learn their own language and also foreign languages by this method. If a German, for example, wants to learn English it will help him to perceive that the English language, far more than German, is based on opposites, or antonyms.

> It is more instructive to show the fact of opposition than to try to explain it in words. By such symbols we can help children learn to use words readily.[11]

Scientific, social and educational contexts raise the question if an ideal artificial language (in this case a visual language) will ever succeed. In some cases it does, e.g. in corporate business culture and in global navigation and information design. According to Umberto Eco (A Theory of Semiotics, 1976) pictograms are quite limited in terms of verbal tenses, adverbs or prepositions. If we look at Neurath's pictograms, further contextual explanations are needed and their usefulness becomes rather confined in larger historical and ethno-cultural contexts.

Semiotically speaking, the concept of "speaking signs" confuses images with signs. According to Peirce a sign is not the image of an object; in fact it has a syntactic, a pragmatic and a semantic dimension. Signs take the form of words, images, sounds, odors, flavors, acts or objects, but such things have no intrinsic meaning and become signs only when we invest them with meaning. 'Nothing is a sign unless it is interpreted as a sign,' declares Peirce.

From today's perspective, Otto Neurath's postulate on unlimited information acquisition gains new actuality in the age of the World Wide Web. Thus the conclusion he drew from the pragmatic value of visual mediated information asking for active interpretation is that direct perception no longer holds the better epistemic credibility. In brief, the way we construct our worldview is a symbolic construction.

2 *Mirror Worlds:* The Universe in a Box?

A highly-reflective model of Earth's visible and intangible aspects has been outlined by David Gelernter (1991) in his book "Mirror Worlds". As the title makes clear, the book's central metaphor is the computer as a mirror of the world. Gelernter suggests that the progress of computing will inevitably produce a single vast, distributed computer system containing a complete mirror image of the whole of reality. Gelernter's predictions of the "downloadable" world, the digital mirror of our reality, will permit individuals to investigate reality without leaving home, simply by "traveling" in the digital mirror:

> Capturing the structure and present status of an entire company, university, hospital, city or whatever in a single (obviously elliptical, high-level) sketch is a hard but solvable research problem. The picture changes subtly as you watch, mirroring changes in the world outside. But for most purposes, you don't merely sit and stare. You zoom in and poke around, like an explorer in a miniature sub. (ibid.: 15)

However, Gelernter's apotheosis of the emerging data-centered view of computing emanates from the realm of human control over nature, i.e. to transform fractious nature into a human one, to domesticate frightful elements, and to predict and to make manageable the power of nature with the aid of the binary code. Hence, a parallel and synthetic world emerges out of human imagination, which pretends to be more human than hostile in nature.

Gelernter is well aware of the privacy and data surveillance concerns that computers have raised, and much of his thoughts are concerned with the nature of public space in the era of the mirror world. One purpose of the Mirror World is to repair social fragmentation by making it possible to grasp the world as a totality through its computer representation. In search of making available what in fact was always available in principle, Gelernter refers to this form of understanding as "topsight", meaning a far-overhead vantage point, a bird's eye view that should reveal how the parts fit together.

If the real mirror world tech trend is towards increased data inputs, which means the proliferation of global sensors, the leading social trend may be efforts of the powerful to control access to the most useful new information. Mirror worlds are democratizing and pluralizing only to the extent that everyone has access to and can annotate them. Gelernter, in response to fears that computers are necessarily instruments of social control through surveillance, argues that the Mirror World will make it possible for ordinary citizens to turn that same power of surveillance back against the state:

> Mirror World is some huge institution's moving, true-to-life mirror image trapped inside a computer—where you can see and grasp it whole. The thick, dense, busy sub-world that encompasses you is also, now, an object in your hands. A brand new equilibrium is born. (ibid.: 3)

If this access is restricted, citizens can easily become instruments of state or corporate control. As long as this is seen as a socially-undesirable outcome, much political effort will go into finding ways to maintain and equalize access.

However, Gelernter's vision goes hand-in-hand with much of the overtly articulated motivation for pervasive computerization in contemporary industrial society, which, simply put, is trying to reproduce the whole world as digital entities. His optimism about this vision, though, is difficult to evaluate. One approach would be to accept the metaphor and dispute his sense of proportion: Mirror Worlds, while increasing the capacity of citizens to conduct computer-mediated surveillance against the powerful, might be held to increase the already vastly greater capacity of the powerful to conduct surveillance of their own. But this argument, while perhaps accurate, is not particularly compelling.

In again approaching the mirror metaphor we have to look more deeply into questions of mediation between reality and digital representations. From the standpoint of mainstream media theory, the media should reflect reality, truth and objectivity without distortion, from a critical standpoint, even though a mirror is about subjectivity and objectivity, looking at and looking through at the same time. Looking through presupposes the notion of another world behind the mirror: a vast spectrum of illusion and disillusion. We can either explore unprecedented prospects of our imaginary world, or we painfully realize that we were just unobtrusively observed from the other side of a two-way mirror.

From Lacan's perspective (1997/1966), the mirror is an image of coherence—of what makes the world and our place as complete subjects in it make sense. It becomes a process of identification of our internal self with that external image. The mirror stage thus represents the infant's first encounter with subjectivity, with spatial relations, with an external sense of coherence, and with a sense of "I" and "You." This mirror reflection provides a source of feedback that allows us to adjust our presentation in order to convey what we want to project.

However, if we are talking about media, perception, and representation, we cannot pass off the symbolic-real-imaginary triad of Jacques Lacan's three psychoanalytic orders, developed during a series of lectures in the 1950's. In our attempt at worldview construction, we seek out (or avoid) the Real World; we have Imaginary Friends; we experience Symbolic Moments.

The Imaginary in Lacan's work is the space in which the relation between the ego and its images is developed. Charles S. Peirce aligns the imaginary with the "icon"—an image which is "understood" with no (or little) mediation, whereas for Saussure the imaginary becomes the "signified", the concept symbolized arbitrarily by a sign.

The Real in Lacanian theory becomes that which resists representation, that is pre-mirror, pre-imaginary, pre-symbolic—that cannot be symbolized—and that loses its "reality" once it is symbolized (made conscious) through language. Friedrich Kittler (1999) uses the gramophone as an example: it records all the scrambled fragmentation of the "real" that is in fact aligned with sound – as opposed to word and image – before this is edited into a coherent picture in other forms like film. In a sense, the real is everything that is not media but that informs all media.

The Symbolic, the subject's relationship with the symbolic, is the heart of Lacanian psychoanalysis. The emergence of symbolic structures is an essential feature of the human transition from nature to culture. Although the exchange of signifiers in speech is an obvious example of symbolic exchange, Lacan's symbolic is not simply synonymous with language and should be understood as comprising the entire domain of culture. The symbolic dimension of language is that of the signifier: a dimension in which elements have no positive existence but are constituted purely by virtue of their mutual differences (see also Peirce's "Symbol", Saussure's "Signifier").

However, the concept of the "mirror world", the "digital realm" whose origin traces back to Descartes' mathematical model[1] of the world, does not provide a satisfying answer to the questions of how human-machine interaction can co-evolve in parallel to our cognitive-emotional capacities to navigate between "real" reality and "virtual" reality. Virtual world realities are entirely computer-generated simulations, which do not mimic nature but illusiveness. In fact, virtual worlds are models of fictive worlds based on digital technology interfusing imagination, simulation and reality. Hence, virtual worlds are dependent on the viewer, who acts at the interfaces of real and simulated worlds. They are computer-controlled and -generated environments that respond to human ideas and needs and which are undetermined and not calculable. Simulations of human imagination can lead to both directions: either to determination of imaginations, or to opening determinations through imaginations.

The term "virtual", though, comprises a whole set of differing connotations and denotations. Gilles Deleuze (1994), for example, uses the term virtual to refer to something that every object carries with it, which is neither its reality nor merely what it could have been, but rather what it is imagined to be. "Virtual" is therefore taken to mean a potential state that could become actual. "Virtual" is not opposed to "real" but opposed to "actual," whereas "real" is opposed to "possible."

The prototypical case is a reflection in a mirror: it is already there, whether I am here to see it; it is not waiting for any kind of actualization. Whichever metaphor you ascribe to digital representations or simulations will not suffice to fully understand the fundamental principles of digital information and its contexts.

Eye in the Sky?

Imagine you are sitting in an airplane looking out the window from an altitude of 10 000m watching a company crop circle logo that softly fades out of your visual field. The surface of the earth could thus turn into a gigantic canvas spanning and defining the globe as the ultimate and all-encompassing super sign. In a certain sense the existing and visible traces on earth caused by nature and human civilization can be assembled as a single, symbolic super-string of human artifacts. One prevalent pattern we are able to identify from the sky are the colorful graduations of squared field patterns, the scattered formations of human settlement. From the standpoint of an observer watching the surface of the earth from the sky, the repository of shapes and figures we cognitively map appears rather confined and simple in comparison to the chaotic and complex forms of nature. From such a high distance perception and cognition of spatial characteristics such as height and depth is barely possible, and the surface underneath my seat dissolves into emblematic flat land.

The sight from the sky, at least as a mental concept in human evolution, must have existed already long ago. The crop circle project of an enthusiastic student group from Oregon state university which depicted the Firefox web browser logo at a final diameter of 220 feet in an unharvested field pursued the idea of making their passion for Firefox visible from space. Behind the challenge of planning and realizing the crop circle stood at least the option of being photographed by one of the Google earth cameras (Fig. 1).

For my part this kind of intervention is a perfect example of how playfully visual communication can be applied across media, time & space, cultures and (in)visible borders. At first glance the whole project conveys the compelling aesthetics of the crop circle phenomenon, which was observed in its current form after notable appearances in England in the late 1970's. Early examples of crop circles were usually simple circular patterns of various sizes that changed gradually into more and more elaborate and complex geometric patterns. Later formations up to the present appear to be based on other principles, natural sciences and mathematics designs, including fractals and elements of three-dimensional objects, culminating in spectacular images of cube-shaped structures.

An important attempt to demystify and disperse any kind of speculation on extraterrestrial draftsmanship were undertaken by two New Hampshire-based artists already in 1978 whose simple circle sets attracted the interest of scientists worldwide. One of the most prominent successors became the UK-based artists Circlemakers.org, who have been asked to create numerous crop circles since the mid 1990's for movies, TV shows, music videos, adverts and PR stunts.

But what makes the student project appealing is the concept of speculating with an audience that is not physically present, addressing an anonymous spectatorship that could eventually participate in the process of making and documenting the project, depending on the satellite's position and the display of information via internet access. Thus the observers are no longer gallery or museum visitors; instead the crop logo or any other sign on the surface of the earth intentionally made for a bird's eye-view is recorded by an invisible "eye" in the sky, the satellite camera, which simultaneously embodies an electronic spectator, image producer and collector.

In contrast to early satellite art projects in the 1970's, which were intentionally conceived to investigate the possibilities and limitations of technologies to create and augment new contexts, environments, and scale for telecollaborative arts (e.g. Satellite Arts Project '77, "A Space With No Geographical Boundaries"), the last decade has seen convergent network technologies becoming a popular playground for sharing audiovisual content, ideas, and interests driven by a common impulse of attentiveness and authenticity. With the rise of web-based communication, the realization of participatory media culture has come in close proximity to its visionary ancestors in the 1920's and 30's: to set the very communication process beyond the realm of mass communication, acknowledging thus a wider field of practice where the communication process is addressed not only in representative terms ("for the people"), but in participatory terms as well ("from the people").

The crop circle project is an endeavor to put emphasis on creation and production—as well as on the process of the communication practice itself and its manifestations of empowerment, in symbolic and reflexive terms. What becomes important in this specific context is the mediation process rather than the media themselves. Accordingly, media practices must be evaluated in a broader context, that of contesting the dominant conditions of media power, its symbolic boundaries and hierarchies. It is the concentration of symbolic power, the long-term impacts of the representations of the social world, that media institutions circulate and which in return alternative media practices contest, declaring the right of their agents to share in

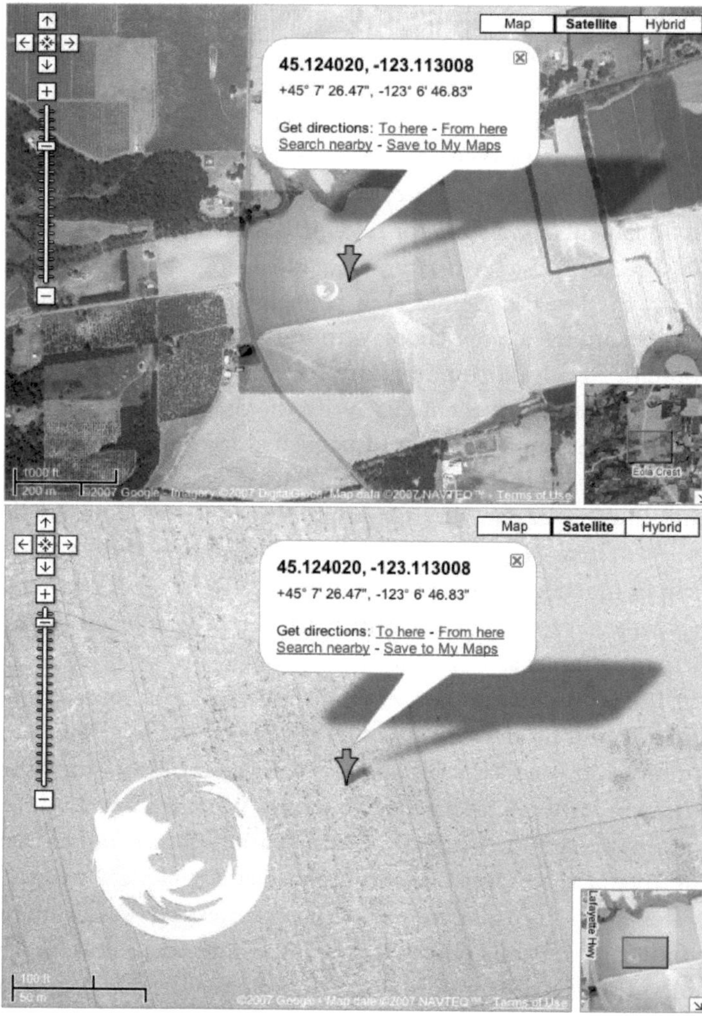

1 Firefox Logo, Google Earth

society's resources for representing itself. This does not necessarily involve our own media production resources; rather they are activities that are articulated on the very limits of a mediation process, within the frame of mainstream media outputs, challenging the operations of media power, as well as, in relation to the media frame, contesting its very constitution.

The extension of the spectrum of alternative media in terms of encompassing instances of empowerment in reflexive as well as in symbolic terms has shifted interest to the "agents" of these practices and the way social actors are engaged with and in these practices. From this perspective, and drawing on the field of reception, increasing attention has been dedicated to the user dimension, given the fact that alternative media activists represent in a sense the most active segment of the so-called "active audience".

Using the example of the crop circle project, we can observe tendencies eliciting a new generation of creative commons, whose diverse adoptions of media production, reception and perception have emerged in flexible alliances of producers and audiences: "media producers" become "media users" and vice versa. Thereby profound understanding of the interrelatedness between disruptive technologies and their contextual application occurs through heterogeneous user groups inducing a new era of media democratization, insofar as the primary source of information—in the case of the Google Map example—acquires its images from a wide range of both commercial and public sources. Despite recent security concerns raised primarily by the companies and governmental agencies that gather and distribute the images, Google's ambitious mission contributes to the pursuit of an all-encompassing world representation.

From Dymaxion to Google Earth

Think global, act local Buckminster Fuller

In 1927 Buckminster Fuller, an educator, engineer, architect, author, cartographer and futurist, set out to develop the world's most accurate two-dimensional world map. He wished to provide a view of the whole Earth at once which would have the ability to reveal major trends in world affairs and show the shortest air routes between land masses. Fuller predicted even then that global travel would shift from the sea to the sky.

Buckminster Fuller proposed to cover the surface of the globe with 4-D towers, delivered by Zeppelin to remote locations. The plan was a proposal for an "omni-directional transportation device", to allow people to reach their homes by means of jets (Fig. 2).

In his privately circulated draft entitled 4D, Fuller actually described the ten-deck houses shown here as "stepping stone, world airline maintenance crew environment controls", the idea being that, if appropriately distributed around the globe, they could serve as maintenance stations for planes on great circular air routes. Fuller was convinced that his plan for mass-produced housing would render city-dwellings obsolete. The 4D-transport, which later developed into the dymaxion automobile, was initially intended as a private vehicle suited for this new, decentralized human condition. Its primary role would be for flight between island dwellings. Fuller's Dymaxion map (the term "Dymaxion" is contracted from DYnamic MAXimum tensION) has many advantages over all of the other types of projections that render the 3D spherical globe as a 2D flat map. The Dymaxion Map (Fig. 3) is the only flat map of the entire surface of the earth that reveals our planet as it really is, an island in one ocean with no visible distortion of the relative shapes and sizes of the land areas, and with no splitting of any continents. Among its characteristics are these:[1]

– The proportions of all parts of the globe are rendered close to their true relative size.
– The Dymaxion map has no 'right way up'. Fuller always argued that in this universe there is no 'up' or 'down', only 'in' and 'out'. Gravitational forces of the stars and planets created 'in', meaning 'towards the gravitational centre', and 'out', meaning 'away fom the gravitational centre'. Similarly 'north' and 'south' could not be interpreted as 'up' and 'down', or 'superior' and 'inferior', which is the orientation of all other map projections.
– The Dymaxion map does not perpetuate the cultural bias that is part of all other world map projections. The cultural and economic 'north/south' divide is reinforced by the north-up-superior/south-down-inferior presentation of all other world maps.
– There is no one 'correct' view of the global map. Peeling the triangular faces of the icosahedron apart in one way results in a icosahedral net that shows an almost contiguous land mass comprising all of the earth's continents - not groups of continents divided by oceans. Peeling the solid apart in a different way presents a view of the world dominated by connected oceans surrounded by land.

Fuller's intent was to emphasize how important it was to "find effective ways for all humanity to see total Earth, [because] nothing could be more prominent in all the trending of all humanity today than the fact that we are soon to become world humans."[2]

The powerful image he developed allowed viewers to study the total synergetic significance of AirOcean economies and alternative strategies for integrating all phases and states of energy resources towards the highest operative advantage of all people.

The computer-assisted information/communication revolution has greatly enhanced our ability to store and transmit vast quantities of reliable data on social, environmental and economic trends. The opportunity before us is to convey this information without bias and distortion and in ways that allow ordinary people to visually grasp and intuitively understand the current predicament of the human experiment.

By using the Dymaxion Map in combination with the enormous database resources and computer graphics available today, it is now highly feasible to accurately and clearly display the inventory of world resources, trends and needs in multiple dimensions. Only an accurate visual tool such as this can enable us to better see and forecast how human activity and other natural phenomena affect the prospects of delivering high standards of living for all people on an ecologically sustainable basis.

The cartography of the world increasingly flows into the cartography of the internet. With satellite photos one can get a bird's-eye view of anyone's home, yard or street. The latest technologies allow you to search satellite/aerial photos by coordinates such as latitude and longitude or by specific addresses. You can view cars parked in someone's driveway, and with infrared photos you can even view people inside a house or cars parked in anyone's garage. It is indisputable that the inherent dichotomy between civilian and state control, people's human-

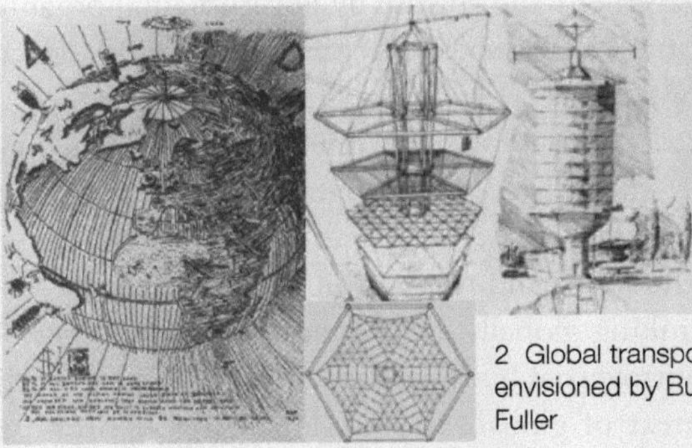

2 Global transportation net, envisioned by Buckminster Fuller

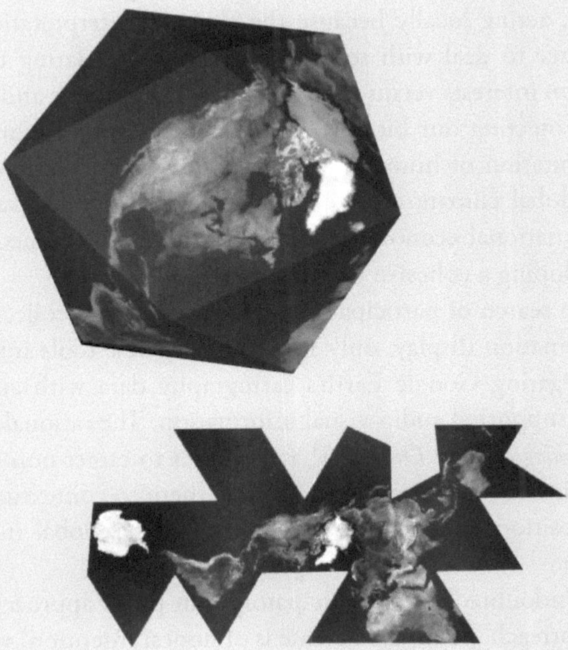

3 The Dymaxion Map

itarian engagement and misuse by governmental organizations leads to distrust and suspicion regarding any kind of mass-mediated information.

Admittedly, the wired and interconnected data map represented by the mirror world data spaces today correspond with some of the ideas Buckminster Fuller strived for in response to the needs and responsibilities of humanity on planet earth. “Thinking globally, acting locally” has however become a rather controversial buzzword revealing major contradictions in the context of globalization. Globalizing environmentalist and futurist movements have thus reinterpreted thinking globally, acting locally because the changed interpretation helps its user to deal with several contradictions relating to global system interests versus individual or local interests and the goal of protecting our biosphere versus expanding economies and exploitation of human and natural resources. Current debate on global climate change policy provides a good example of how national economic interests collide with the necessity of developing a cohesive world climate policy.

In search of participatory, multilayered data collection and information display, only recently were new tools introduced aggregating Google Earth's cartography data with additional user-supported audio-visual information. The rationale behind the *Google Earth Outreach*[3] approach is to target non-profit or public benefit groups and to enable them to contextualize and to position their work more visibly on the global info landscape.

Undoubtedly, the participatory non-profit approach Google Outreach attempts to create is of honest intention, yet in the case of the genocide in Darfur, several endeavors to raise public consciousness on the human disaster came far too late.

> From the point of view of the hopes raised by two of the optimistic lessons from Rwanda, the response of the "international community" to the crisis in Darfur can only be considered a giant, tragic set-back. It is not too much to say that Darfur shows that only the first despairing lesson - the bottomless cynicism and self-interest of the major powers - remains valid, while the hopes have been largely destroyed.[4]

It is the mission of the *U.S. Holocaust Memorial Museum's Genocide Prevention Mapping Initiative* to confront threats of genocide and related crimes against humanity today, a legacy hauntingly echoed in Nobel Peace Laureate Eli Wiesel's message, "A memorial unresponsive to the future would violate the memory of the past".[5] Top of the partnership agenda between Google Earth and the Museum is constantly updated information in a visual, compelling and timely format to serve as an effective vehicle for public outreach and education about genocide and related crimes against humanity.

In the course of globally acting humanitarian aid initiatives, several non-governmental organizations are implementing collaborative and dynamic ways for communities to come together, share critical information, and help citizens to protect their rights. Although rapid access to satellite imagery increases the chance to publicly monitor certain areas at risk, political and military interest groups will remain the commanders in both censored and uncensored satellite imaging provision.

Participatory co-creation of global info maps entails both: a potential risk of arbitrariness and unreliability, and a multi-perspective aggregation of individual information and knowledge resources. The criteria of objectivity in news reporting became obsolete long ago, and the adherent promises of authenticity as being a necessary corrective in participatory media culture have not yet been fulfilled. Any kind of amalgamation of hybrid real and virtual world data feed is prone to falsification and deception.

In future the same number of people engaged in collaborative feeding of globally connected databases will be used to spend time on controlling and verifying the countless number of individually submitted lifelogging information chunks.

Long before Google Earth came into existence, Geographic Information Systems (GIS) were in place for capturing, managing, analyzing, and displaying all forms of geographically referenced information. GIS organizes geographic data such that a person reading a map can select data necessary for a specific project or task. Depending on the scope of application, selected data sets from both commercial vendors or government agencies can be added as data layers to a map so that, for example, a social analyst can retrieve localizable information on residents' education levels, ages, and employment status.

The problem with high-quality GIS data stems from high costs for development and maintenance. Due to shrinking government budgets, rising deficits, and a strong political aversion to tax increases, public agencies are adopting entrepreneurial methods for funding (not only) their GIS databases. Yet, the sale of public data by government agencies threatens to restrict free access to so-called public sector information, which is considered raw material for added-value services and additional business opportunities. If we take into account the enormous amount of supposedly publicly accessible information stored in national databases, such as financial and business information; legal and administrative information; patents; and tourist and traffic information, it becomes obvious that the re-use of digital public resources will create an impermeable jungle of legislation, regulations, policies, and guidelines that concurrently support deregulation and misuse of personal data.

Info mapping, whether it is on a global, national or regional scale, always implies a certain vulnerability to sensitive information that is not meant to be shared with the public. Google Earth Outreach as a kind of participative "Geographical Info Wiki" has the potential to engage a critical mass of users who closely cooperate with NGOs and public services to create—at the very least—an alternative approach driven by non-commercial interests.

Visual Evidence: Aesthetics of (Un)Certainty?

Why do we take, collect and share such enormous amounts of mediated worldviews? What are we going to do with this overwhelming bulk of digital representations? Is it a re-assurance of our own reality construction in the multiverse? The multiverse model of the world does not only reflect the new technologically determined experiences of time and space, not only new cosmological principles, but also new concepts of social reality and "conditio humana". The world of media and technology creates several modal parallel worlds in the "real" world.

In my attempt towards a visual-evidence based analysis of some of the most prevalent global connectivity phenomena based on mobile imaging and ubiquitous data exchange, I will start with a short narrative that would also support in that specific context the idea of identity construction in interrelated spatial/temporal, socio-cultural and media-technical contexts.

I am sitting and waiting for the next connecting flight. A con-

> glomeration of ideas circulates in my mind, whilst watching the manifold outdoor activities through the airport building windows.
> The frozen glass tripartite in front of me is framed like a triptych containing live images. Some elements within the framed reality are static; a few of them are moving around vertically and horizontally on the imaginary screen.
> A plane wipes from the right to left and vanishes in undefined time and space. Three-dimensional perception interferes with two-dimensional invisible traces, markers and ephemeral reflections on the glass canvas.
> What if the fragile and transparent wall broke into a thousand pieces? … The glass is just a weak membrane between reality and illusion, and I am sitting and waiting.

How do I gain a grip on the essence of my thoughts that motivated me to reflect on certain phenomena exactly at that time, situation and space? I start sketching and recalling fragmentary visual mnemonics (memory aids) but I cannot exactly remember the spatial dimensions and details of the furnished environment inside the Schiphol airport building (Fig. 4):

> Yesterday I was in London and today I am in Paris.
> I am shooting images with my thinking eyes. Images are floating thoughts, unless I capture some of them in manifested form.
> I search for thoughts, stimuli and sometimes reality.
> The process of visually reconstructing mental images has just begun.

The search function on flickr.com, one of the largest public and community-driven photo repositories on the web, allows

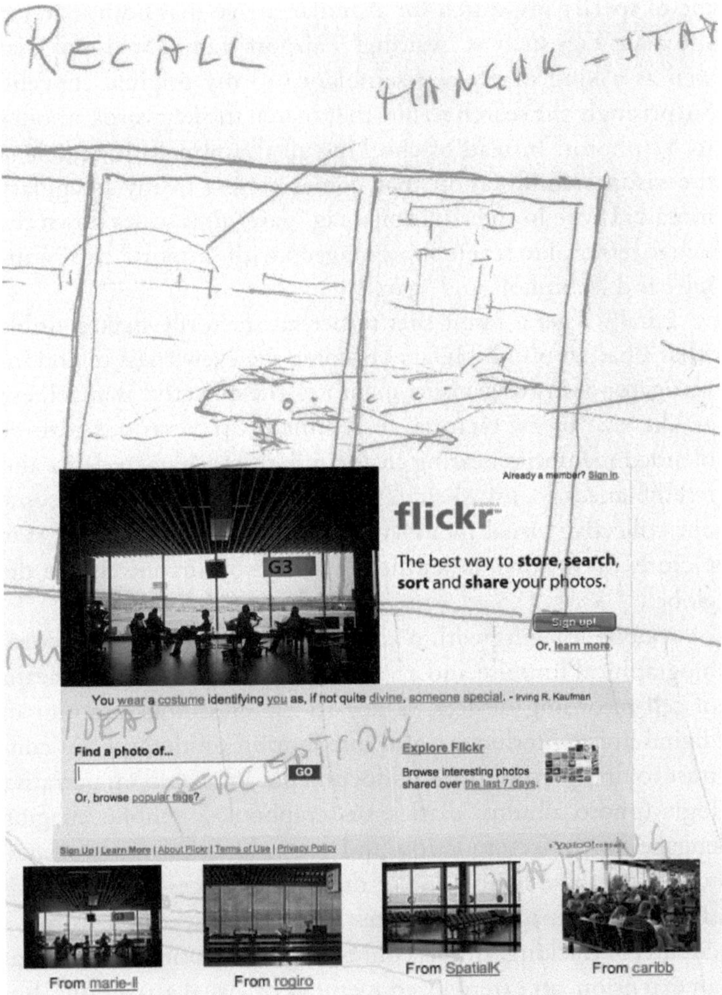

4 The global database has become our collective visual memory

me to specify my search for a similar image that both matches the main tags such as "waiting", "airport", and "Schiphol", as well as a kind of visual resemblance to my original concept. Surprisingly the search results that match the keywords amount to 57 photos. Instead of checking all thumbnails in search of the visual manifestation that comes closest to my imaginary mosaic, I type in the additional tag "gate" that scales down the image retrieval to seven photos tagged with "airport" and "waiting" and "schiphol" and "gate".

Finally I get a result that rather satisfactorily makes visible what I had in mind. Hence I become the eyewitness to and investigator of my own visual memory. The objective is to achieve a "likeness" of my pictorial record made up of various parts or blended memories bearing close similarities, characteristics and resemblances to my sketch. The global database has become our collective visual memory. It makes no difference if I take pictures on my own or let them be taken by anyone else on the globe.

Mobile imaging with a camera phone, driven by an autobiographical impulse and a yearning for authenticity by means of self-recording devices, is key to the enormous amount of digital image production and distribution on the web. In contrast to first-person forms of documentation based on narrative logic (photo albums, diaries, or scrapbooks), mobile imaging engages with accumulation and recombination as associated with a database logic. One of the consequences of this shift is that mobile imaging implicates its practitioners in assortative circuits of tracking. In this context digital shooting functions as an extension, an externalized memory of visual attractions, but it also revises the impetus self-reflexiveness. The apparent coercion into continuous imaging, a result of the device (potentially) always being in hand, drives a persistent and continuous awareness: an alerted attention towards potential shooting.

The act of self-evidencing leads to never-before-seen image production, comprising an ever-expanding visual statistical archive. Photo shooting by mobile phone engages the practitioners to comprehensively participate in the circulation of images and tracking functions. Considering the exorbitant number of images produced, dispersion of accumulated photo streams are rather approached across series than in distinct personal episodes. The logic behind these collections of images suggests that databases do not tell stories, they do not have a beginning or an end, and do not have any sequence (thematically or formally). They contain a collection of items, each having the same significance as any other. Databases, on the other hand, (re)define the narrative form so that it can be construed as a particular trajectory through a space of possibilities and meanings. Manovich (2001: 225) treats narrative and database as two conflicting representational impulses with the former emphasizing a cause and effect chain of events and the latter a list of disparate elements. This theoretical tension between narrative and database is manifested in Soft Cinema films as two competing interpretive systems through which the spectator can impose coherence onto the films. In order to better understand the soft cinema approach, it is necessary to describe its core ideas:[6]

> – *Algorithmic Cinema.* Using systems of rules, software controls both the layout of the screen (number and positions of frames) and the sequences of media elements which appear in these frames.
>
> – *Macro-cinema.* Soft Cinema imagines how moving images may look when the Net matures, and when unlimited band-

width and very high resolution displays become the norm.
– *Multimedia cinema.* In Soft Cinema video is used as only one type of representation among others: 2D animation, motion graphics, 3D scenes, diagrams, etc.
– *Database Cinema.* The media elements are selected from a large database to construct a potentially unlimited number of different narrative films.

Manovich applies the transcoding principle in his discussion of the differences betwen the symbolic forms of narrative and database, and the tendency for new media towards the database form. As a result, the dynamic WWW conveys an anti-narrative logic, resulting in a collection, not a story.

In the hope of resolving this dichotomic relationship and refining these concepts towards a *user driven logic*, I will argue that all media experience shifts between two separate states of reception: immediacy & hypermediation, a dynamic balance for which Bolter and Grusin (1999) use the term "remediation".

Hypermediation helps to sustain repeated viewings. The emerging role of the new generation of web applications enables the participants to associate "tags" or "labels", "keywords", or "categories" with the media objects they encounter. This activity is transmedial as it includes text (emails, news, blogs, wiki entries), images, audio, video, and hyperlinks. The mix of embedded media components thus creates a heterogeneous texture and multiple views. Immediacy, understood as a tendency towards transparent immersion, occurs in continuous imaging when taking, publishing and sharing pictures occurs as a seamless experience.

For all that, the question is to what extent personal tagging contributes to database and narrative convergence. In some respect tagging resembles the traditional criterion for a narrative, implying the co-creating role of an actor, narrator and director merging into the "tagger" who creates connections between the objects, and privileging some objects over others.

Tagging, by applying alternative parts of speech indicating emotional expressions such as "wish lists", "likes", "dislikes", verbs (to-read, to-do), and reflexive pronouns, can be understood as narrative concepts for creating paths through databases, which is reminiscent of Walter Benjamin's thoughts on collecting and implicitly creates an autobiographical narrative. The collector who unpacks his old books and restores his library does not simply "own" or memorialize the past but also disrupts the present: his collecting and re-collecting make immediately visible and relevant, against his will, what was forgotten, past, or dead.[7] Accordingly, Benjamin suggests that the subjective act of filtering creates a special meaning, denoted by the relationship between the collector and the collected. Tag clouds, from the standpoint of user experience, commonly consist of two elements: a collection of linked tags shown in varying fonts and colors to indicate frequency of use or importance, and a title to indicate the context of the collection of tags. Flickr's tags page is the iconic example of the first generation tag cloud.

An important usage pattern for tagging is the so-called *folksonomy*—a term coined by Thomas Vander Wal. Folksonomy is the result of personal free tagging of information and objects for one's own retrieval. As folksonomies develop in Internet-mediated social environments, users can discover (generally) who created a given folksonomy tag and see the other tags that this person created.

Alongside the social web developments, the database logic pursued by Manovich and Kratky in their soft cinema project entails closure inasmuch as video-/photo sharing tools, videoblogging and lifelogging open up new possibilities to make content granular and mashable: tagging scenes and shots, linking between them, making it easy to remix content at the level of the smallest possible unit. This non-linear and non-closure approach to a collage of content, a collage of contributors leading to multiple outcomes/interpretations following the database form of the web, could become something new. As there is no "last page of the Internet", the aesthetics of "YOUser cinema" would not be framed by a need for closure, and every movement towards participatory media culture would open up new trajectories rather than shut them down.

Data Visualizations

In his renowned book "Envisioning information" (1990), Edward Tufte poses the fundamental question, "how are we to present the rich visual world of experience and measurement on mere flatland?" (ibid.: 9) Charts, diagrams, graphs, tables, guides, instructions, directories and maps comprise an enormous accumulation of material, whose display in a functional and aesthetic way are the main challenges in "cognitive art" (Philip Morrison). Tufte calls in this context for specific design skills at the intersections of image, word, number and art.

The roots of the graphic portrayal of quantitative information reach into histories of thematic cartography, statistical graphics, and data visualization, which are intertwined with each other. They also connect with the rise of statistical thinking up through the 19th century, and developments in technology into the 20th century (see Chapter 1). The principle questions concerning visual consequences govern the design, editing, analysis and critique of data representations and can be similarly applied to analog and digital forms of data representation. In order to understand the digital data not only as visual representations on the screen, we need to discern firstly the algorithmic characteristics of image processing, and secondly the dynamics of data mining, meta data and its semantics.

Increasing computer capacity has led to tremendous amounts of data collections in almost all socially relevant networks and organizations. From flight plans to forecast maps, from tomography to robot simulations, from global info maps to artistic data sculpture, this digital information can only be fully understood if information visualization, data mining and graphic design are jointly employed. Ben Fry opts in this context for "a singular process titled Computational Information Design". (Frey 2004: 17)

Data visualization[8] or scientific visualization is a subject in computer science that deals with the use of interactive, sensory (audiovisual) representations of abstract data to reinforce cognition, hypothesis building and reasoning. In other words, data visualization is the graphical presentation of information, with the goal of providing the viewer with a qualitative understanding of the information contents. My concern is to concentrate mainly on visual data representations, although we should not exclude sonic representations that hold similar importance in scientific contexts, for example as applied in volcano research. Thereby geophysical information on seismic movements are transformed into audible sound waves using the process of data sonification.[9] Consequently, sound waves can be analyzed for patterns of behavior and self similarities in eruption dynamics that can then be used to predict the future activity of a volcano.

In its early days computer graphics had been used to study scientific problems, but the lack of graphics power often limited its usefulness. The historical roots of emphasizing visualization traces back to 1987 with the special issue of Computer Graphics on Visualization in Scientific Computing, and last but not least recognized with the first Ars Electronica awards ("Goldene Nica") in the categories of computer graphics and digital music (Peter Gabriel and Jean-Claude Risset).[10] From this year forward, the spreading of computer visualization in scientific and artistic fields of application met its challenge, principally in three areas: first, efficient graphics algorithms for displaying the data; second, novel special-purpose graphics hardware; and third, interactive techniques for graphically manipulating the data at close to video rates.[11]

The enormous amount of data and its growing fields of application required in the course of time classification schemes that involved selecting, transforming and representing abstract data in a form that facilitated human interaction for exploration and understanding. As a result, the user was enabled to modify the visualization in real-time, yet under the premises of meaningfully interpreting an unparalleled perception of patterns and structural relations on the basis of abstract data accumulations.

Besides the necessity of understanding some of the main principles of database logic, it appears helpful to firstly gain deeper insights into computer-generated visualizations from the viewpoint of a consistent methodological classification (cf. Lenger & Eppler[12])—to at least mention a few of them:

a) Data visualization: Visual representation of quantitative data in schematic form (e.g. histograms, bar charts, tables etc.);

b) Information visualization (Fig. 5): The use of interactive visual representations of data to amplify cognition. This means

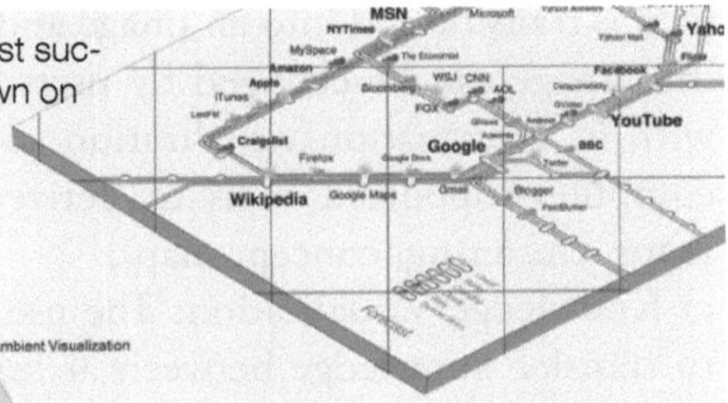

5 "Web Trend", the 200 most successful websites pinned down on the Tokyo Metro Map

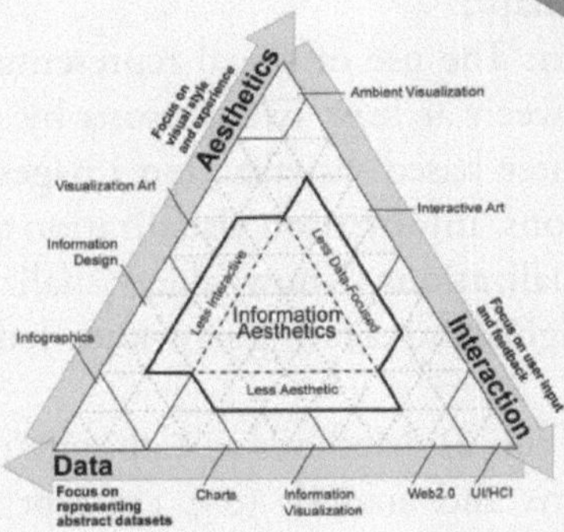

6 Lau & Vande Moere: Model of Information Aesthetics

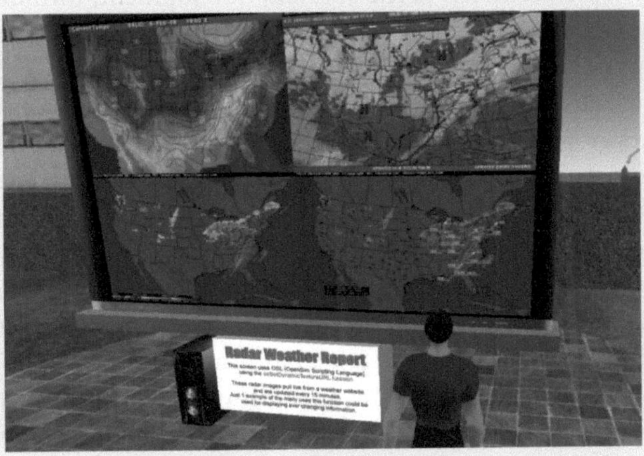

7 Open Simulator Virtual Worlds Server Weather Report

data is transformed into an image and mapped to screen space. The image can be changed by users as they proceed working with it. Information visualization concentrates on the use of computer-supported tools to derive new insights (e.g. data maps, clustering, concept map).

c) Knowledge Visualization: The use of visual representations to transfer knowledge between at least two persons by using computer and non-computer based visualization images, objects, interactive visualizations, information visualization applications and imaginary visualizations. Knowledge visualization focuses on transferring insights and creating new knowledge in groups.

d) Concept Visualization (Fig. 6): Methods to elaborate qualitative concepts, ideas, plans and analysis (e.g. concept map, communication diagram, flight plan).

e) Strategy Visualization: The systematic use of complementary representations in the analysis, development, formulation, communication and implementation of strategies in organizations (strategy map, stakeholder map, organization chart).

f) Metaphor Visualization: Visual metaphors position information graphically to organize and structure information. They also convey an insight about the represented information through the key characteristics of the metaphor employed (metro map, tree, funnel).

g) Compound Visualization: The complementary use of different graphic representation formats in one single schema or frame (cartoons, knowledge map, learning map).

This list can be optionally adjusted, but coming back to mixed media and (meta)cognitive layers in networked real and virtual environments, we must go a step further by looking at visualization concepts that would allow the actor to experience a multisensoric 3D dataspace. “Escaping Flatland”, as Edward

Tufte suggests, is a challenging design approach: one example uses layering and separation to foster comprehension of multivariate data. Although his approach provides an important basis, it would require several adjustments for virtual spaces such as map, spatial, navigation and game design. What has been already in place for a long time, stereoscopic vision, for example, gains fresh momentum alongside the driving forces of 3D Internet (Open Sim [Fig. 7], Moveable Life etc.), by enabling an immersive stereoscopic projection of a life-size screen covering 180 degrees of vision, connected to the live grid, and tracking the avatar with ultra-wideband emitters. The avatar representing the user is moved according to the positions calculated, and its movement is simultaneously reflected in the live display of the Second Life grid. When the system is set up so that the field of view is at a scale of 1:1 with respect to the user, then the visualization of the avatar representing the user is no longer necessary, as there is a direct correspondence between the scene and the user's proprioception (proprioception provides an awareness of movement and position of the parts of the body.)[13] A similar attempt towards 3D interactive data visualizations deals with a method for point-of-view dependent 3D image projection onto almost any surface using multiple projectors for Virtual/Augmented Reality applications.[14]

Data representations are therefore becoming increasingly adaptable through full body tracking that enables the beholder to interact with the image so that the picture angle synchronously adjusts to the field of vision of the observer. The impression of real sight and interaction with real objects, though they are simulations, should thereby allow the user to discover new data worlds previously invisible.

This leads to facilitation of new kinds of learning experiences that are highly perceptual in nature, and which enable the students to be immersed within a phenomenon in a visual, auditory and haptic manner. Thus virtual environments are suitable places where difficult and abstract models, intangible phenomena or intellectually demanding processes can be modeled and with which students can take part and interact. The idea that students are better able to master, retain and generalize new knowledge when they are actively involved in constructing the knowledge through learning-by-doing owes in part to constructivist thinking, that is, the focus of the learner on thinking about learning.

How did data enter into the art picture, or should we say, what has a telephone to do with a Dadaist hoax that was taken literally by an artist? In the first decades of the twentieth century, the telephone and the radio were for the avant-garde artists of that century symbols of modern communication, by which technology could extend human perception and capabilities. In 1920, in the "Dada Almanac" edited in Berlin by Richard Hülsenbeck, the irreverent proposal was made that a painter could now order pictures by telephone and have them made by a cabinetmaker. It is uncertain whether the constructivist artist Laszlo Moholy-Nagy (1895-1946) read or heard about this provocative statement, yet what is certain is that he considered intellectual motivations as valid as emotional ones in creating art. Therefore it appears plausible that in order to prove the validity of his own assumptions, Moholy-Nagy wrote in 1922,

> I ordered by telephone from a sign factory five paintings in porcelain enamel. I had the factory's color chart before me and I sketched my paintings on graph paper. At the other end of the telephone the factory supervisor had the same kind of paper, divided into squares. He took down the dictated shapes in the

> correct position. (It was like playing chess by correspondence.) One of the pictures was delivered in three different sizes, so that I could study the subtle differences in the color relations caused by the enlargement and reduction.[15]

Whether you seek to analyze them according to communication and information technological aspects, or from the perspective of mechanization, reproduction, authorship, or artistic practice, the "Telephone Pictures" convey some of the paradigmatic principles of modern (concept) art:
– the artwork does not necessarily have to be a physical entity;
– the artwork can be a description or an instruction to be executed by someone else;
– the art work can be produced, transmitted, displayed, reproduced, scaled by different media.

A set of instructions given over the telephone can be described as an algorithm, which underpins the supra-individualism of the Constructivist concept, the existence of objective visual values, independent of the artist's inspiration and his specific art piece. From there it was only a further step towards the first Turing machines in 1936, which were the first simple abstract computational devices intended to help investigate the extent and limitations of what can be computed. Turing was interested in the question of what it means to be computable. Intuitively a task is computable if one can specify a sequence of instructions which when followed will result in the completion of the task. Such a set of instructions is called an effective procedure, or algorithm, for the task.[16]

Consequently, an algorithm is an unambiguous and abstract description of how a specific type of problem is solved. Examples include a food recipe or instructions on how to assemble

Ikea furniture. If algorithms are completely logical and contain all their requirements they can be carried out by a computer and turned into digital data. The function of computers is actually more or less controlled by algorithms: from the control system to the chips, to the software used on top of the control system, and the routines the software is used to perform.

Any work of digital art incorporates a layer of code. Understanding at least the basic nature and language of digital art and its foundation in code-driven or algorithmic processes is an important element in establishing its identity. It is precisely this layer of code and instructions that constitute a conceptional level, which in turn connects to previous artistic work such as Fluxus' and Dada's experiments with formal variations (e.g. concrete poetry) and the conceptional pieces by Duchamp, Cage and Sol LeWitt that are based on the executions of instructions.

Tristan Tzara's generic instructions for writing Dada poems by shuffling the words of a newspaper article can be interpreted as an algorithm—at least from the standpoint of software art proponent F. Cramer:[17]

> To make a Dadaist poem:
> Take a newspaper.
> Take a pair of scissors.
> Choose an article as long as you are planning to make your poem.
> Cut out the article.
> Then cut out each of the words that make up this article and put them in a bag.
> Shake it gently.
> Then take out the scraps one after the other in the order in

which they left the bag.
Copy conscientiously.
The poem will be like you.
And here you are a writer, infinitely original and endowed with a sensibility that is charming though beyond the understanding of the vulgar.

Cramer argues that this poem is effectively an algorithm, a piece of software which may as well be written as a computer program. Conversely, computer language could be applied to generate infinite randomized versions of this Dada poem with optional output.

On the bit-level there is no difference between images and any other data. Images come into existence only at the interface when they appear as something visual. The circulation of images and coding is essentially defined between bits and the screen by algorithms, metadata, formats and protocols.

At the beginning of the 21st century the basics for a new technology were laid in several research laboratories around the globe that allowed entirely new discovery into hitherto invisible worlds. The invention of the scanning tunneling microscope (STM) in 1986 by Binning and Rohrer, for which they earned the Nobel Prize in Physics, made it possible for the first time to make visible the long assumed, but never seen, atomic structure of matter (Fig. 4). We are talking about a micro-world in dimensions of one part in a billion meters, which became immediately experienceable and manipulable. It was even possible to move some molecules around in quantum mechanic experiments.[18] In classical microscopy the maximum resolution was half the wavelength of light, whereas STM permits the observer to actively engage with the nano world, the basis of all

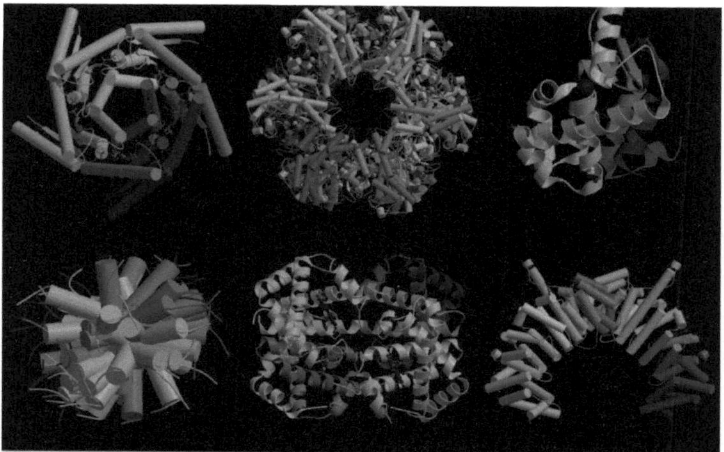

4 Protein Art

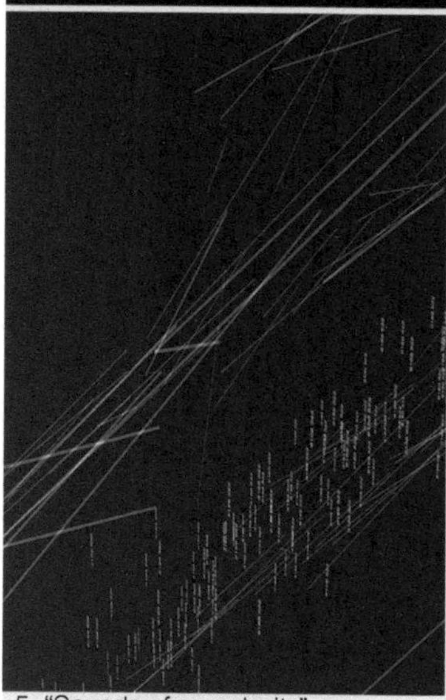

5 "Sounds of complexity",
Plot of 1 second of human brain (EEG) activity

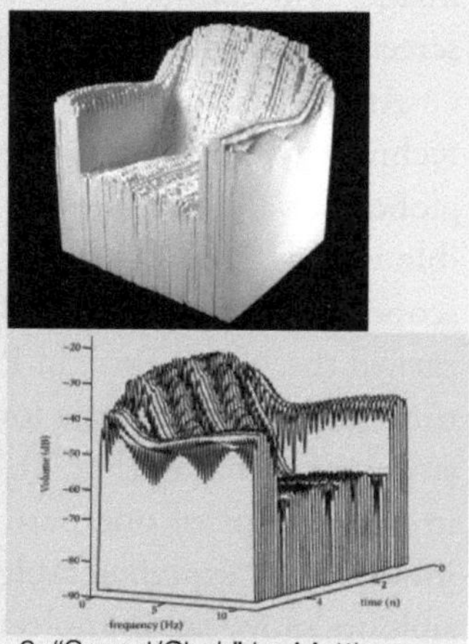

6 "Sound/Chair" by Matthew Plummer Fernandez

(non)living matter.

This new experience of reality coevally poses new questions about its interpretation: between the actual made visible, the billionfold enlarged image, and the object of investigation, the unaffected atomic matter, a multiple transfer process is necessary that takes both objective technical criteria and subjective selection processes into consideration. It is thus legitimate to question what it actually means to talk about "seeing" on an atomic level in view of the fact that we cannot verify our concept of atoms empirically.

Based on the facts given, the fundamental question is if the scanning tunnel microscope is the appropriate medium for our understanding of the nano world, as it deprives our eyes of any immediate view. An alternative suggestion to make experienceable the invisible came from a physician, who experimented with audible structures of atomic configurations. Unlike the eye which assimilates optical impulses linearly, the ear deals with sound logarithmically. As a consequence, a new project called "Atomare Klangwelten" emerged out of the physical experiments in which the crystallographic configurations of the atomic structure were made audible in front of an audience for the first time. The making of something hearable that is in fact inaudible thus suggests according to the "Iconic Turn" an equivalent "Sonic Turn" (Fig. 5, 6).[19]

Coming back to the process of transferring invisible matter into a visible and perceivable form requires several steps of transfer processes. In this context we need to establish a consistent reaction correlation between form, history, perception and content as part of any kind of imaging processing system.

Thereby the subjectivity factor plays an important role considering the selection of images in scientific contexts. Usually after a test arrangement there are several images from one object available which naturally differ slightly in character and quality because the boundary conditions of recording are only partly known and repeatable. A molecule for example could be recorded in different oscillation situations whereas some parts of it remain totally undiscoverable.

Data visualizations of the smallest possible scale particles consistently pose the question of what they actually look like and are thus dependent on individual selection criteria such as likeness, beauty, sharpness. Images are also perceived and interpreted differently by various people according to their previous knowledge, taste, viewing habits and scientific traditions. The way we interpret and conceive our world is certainly owing to a specific cultural predisposition. For example, the prevailing concept of the atom is still driven by Democrit's assumption of a spherical shape, yet we always need to put into perspective the fact that atoms are not visible per se and therefore their forms of representation can be either a formula, a model, or a visual or sonic representation of measured data.
What we then see is that objectivity is relative regarding scientific visualizations.

Science is moving closer to fiction and vice versa: the artificial construction of images resembles more and more intentional artistic contention with regards to scientific phenomena.

3 Lifelogging: A Concept of Sousveillance?

The term "lifelog" refers to augmentation technologies that record and report the intimate states of object- and self-memory, observation, communication, and behavior modeling.

> "A lifelog is conceived as a form of pervasive computing consisting of a unified digital record of the totality of an individual's experiences, captured multimodally through digital sensors and stored permanently as a personal multimedia archive."[1]

Lifelog technologies record and store everyday conversations, actions, and experiences of their users, enabling future replay and aiding remembrance. The emergent interest in the concept of lifelogging stems from the growing capacity to store and retrieve traces of one's life via computing devices. The Metaverse Roadmap concept paper[2] suggests a distinction from Object Lifelogs ("spimes," "blogjects"), which maintain a narrative of use, environment and condition for physical objects. User Lifelogs ("life-caching," "documented lives" etc.) allow people to make similar recordings of their own lives. Both lifelog concepts rely on augmented reality information networks and ubiquitous sensors (Fig. 1, 2).

But what is the impulse, the rationale behind this frantic movement of digital evangelists? Are they aiming at a digital life record that could someday a) replace or complement existing memory preservation practice; b) preserve subjectively noteworthy facts and impressions from a diary or journal; c) retain, like an old-fashioned photo album, scrapbook or home video, images of childhood, loved ones and travels; d) store documents like a cardboard box, time capsule or filing cabinet;

e) record communications data, keystrokes and internet trails like personal computing software?

In addition lifelogs could store data pertaining to health conditions and running statistics, as Nike and Apple introduced in partnership turning shoes into lifelogs and personal trainers, using the iPod and the web. Tens of thousands of runners upload their running statistics daily to an online community.

User lifelogs are becoming increasingly popular and perhaps the most evident early examples are the current generation's widespread use of cell phone cameras to document and share life experiences online. Mobile devices in conjunction with web technologies have created seamless interfaces that facilitate photo taking, annotating, sharing and mobile blogging.

From a technological standpoint lifelogging entails two core functions: collecting aggregated life experiences and sharing them in a collaborative way. Both functions are potentially socially-disruptive, even as they offer capabilities of immediate value to users. In a wider context of social and cultural fulfilment, it is our responsibility to foresee parts of the disruptive behavior or make the technology as adaptive as possible for the end user (community). Here the community aspects of the social web positively impact and accelerate this discussion.

Limitations of human brain capacities to store and retrieve information were put into an informational, technological context at the Bell Labs in the 1980's. The experiments there revealed the remarkable results that human beings remembered very nearly two bits per second under all experimental conditions. Continued over a lifetime, this rate of memorization would produce something over 109 bits, or a few hundred megabytes.[3]

In 1945 Vannevar Bush published an article called "As We May Think" in The Atlantic Monthly. Bush, an American engineer and science administrator known for his work on analog computing, as well as his political role in the development of the atomic bomb during the Second World War, speculated about what work scientists would take up, now that they no longer had to invent weapons. Among other things, he decided that innovations in photography would produce smaller cameras. "The camera hound of the future wears on his forehead a lump a little larger than a walnut," so that he or she could take photographs all day. The problem would be what to do with them. "Consider a future device for individual use, which is a sort of mechanized private file and library, ... it needs a name, and, to coin one at random, 'memex' will do."[4] Memex stood for "memory extender" (Fig. 3).

What Bush called the memex would consist of a desk that had "slanting translucent screens, on which material can be projected for convenient reading." Anything entered into the memex would be saved on microfilm. Bush thought that "if the user inserted 5000 pages of material a day it would take him hundreds of years to fill the repository, so he can be profligate and enter material freely."

The memex user could thus retrieve a book by means of a code and project a book and a photograph on one screen. When he found a congenial collection of material, a trail, he could join it together and save it, or add it to another trail—anticipating what was subsequently read by both Ted Nelson and Douglas Engelbart, and was a factor in their independent formulations of the various ideas that became hypertext.

What has been argued already in Chapter 1, and what deserves specific attention, is the fact that already in 1934, years before Vannevar Bush dreamed of the Memex, decades before Ted Nelson coined the term "hypertext," Paul Otlet was developing the first mechanical database: a rotating, wheel-shaped

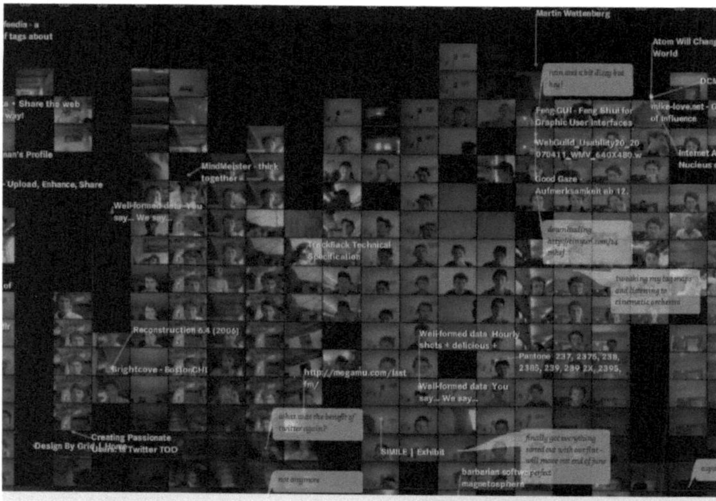

1 Lifelogging= hourly shots from webcam + Twitter posts + delicious bookmarks

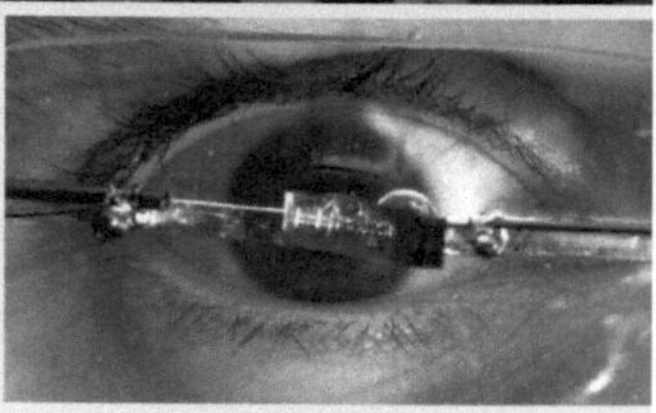

2 Steve Mann's "Wearcam"

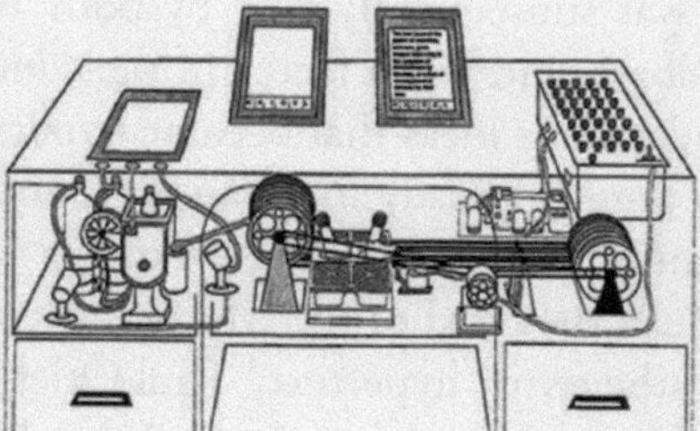

3 Vannevar Bush, "Memex"

desk through which users could browse and annotate millions of index cards. At that time no one could foresee the dynamism of actual knowledge acceleration and its multifaceted effects on data storage, classification and retrieval. Nowadays almost all libraries, museums, archives and public information and knowledge domains are confronted with the complexity of digitizing, contextualizing and delivering cultural heritage within web-based digital resources. Alongside the challenges the semantic web poses to authoring content, structured tagging, ontologies and metadata, the more challenging question will be how all these digital artifacts can be stored, archived and displayed with future media formats as yet unknown. It is thus worthwhile to occasionally ponder the prerequisites of archiving and preserving in the form of a time capsule.

In 1974, the artist Andy Warhol began his own "time capsule"[5] project. This serial work, spanning a thirty-year period from the early 1960's to the late 1980's, consists of 610 standard-sized cardboard boxes, which Warhol, beginning in 1974, filled, sealed and sent to storage. Warhol used these boxes to manage the bewildering quantity of material that routinely passed through his life. Photographs, newspapers and magazines, fan letters, business and personal correspondence, artwork, source images for artwork, books, exhibition catalogs, and telephone messages, along with objects and countless examples of ephemera, such as announcements for poetry readings and dinner invitations, were placed on an almost daily basis into a box kept conveniently next to his desk.

The idiosyncratic and narcissist way Warhol documented himself as a "living art work" represents a drift in emphasis from episodic preservation of the memory of a whole, to informal, continuous preservation of the memory of a single, singular individual. In this respect Warhol's art project can be situated between the quasi-scientific time-capsuling projects of the 20th century and unredeemed technological promises of 21st century “lifelogging”.

In 1998 Gordon Bell, a senior researcher at Microsoft, began digitally capturing his entire life for a project he called *MyLifeBits*, a project to fulfill the Memex vision first posited by Vannevar Bush in 1945. Bell started to scan his old photographs, research documents, and notes, which consequently led him to recording his meetings, phone calls and cataloguing his new photos and movies he saw.

> “It is a system for storing all of one’s digital media, including documents, images, sounds, and videos, built on four principles: (1) collections and search must replace hierarchy for organization (2) many visualizations should be supported (3) annotations are critical to non-text media and must be made easy, and (4) authoring should be via transclusion.”[6]

Every e-mail exchange he had was digitally archived, and he began using the company’s prototype SenseCam, which he wears around his neck, to automatically snap photos throughout the day. Bell manually documents about one gigabyte of information every month, all of which is stored in a searchable database on his PC. He draws from his experiences a future scenario of memory storage on a single device that will automatically create an inventory of the conversations we have, the faces we see and the articles we read. The encoded information would then be tied to communications that are already tracked electronically. Is this a vision of total control, total recall, or radical self-surveillance?

Global Sign Culture

"The man with the master plan is often a woman" (Fig. 4). This particular slogan has, however, taken on a whole set of connotated meanings. One could suggest quite the opposite intention: "The woman with a master plan acts like a man." This text displayed on the gateway at Schiphol airport is an advertising slogan from a Dutch bank. The logo, though not visible in this picture, incorporates irrefutable signified power and status that undeniably adheres to male dominance in business matters. In a sign economy branding transforms recognition into value. At the end of the day, the bank, the bankers are planning your future.

In the United States the "Women's Institute for Financial Education" advocates a bumper sticker with the slogan: "A man is not a financial plan." It is meant to be a call for women to develop a solid plan to secure their financial future and not to leave that responsibility to their husbands or significant others.

Imani Coppola's "masterplan" in her music video "Legend of a Cowgirl" (1997) is a bold feminist statement. The audience however did not fully accept this work because it contrasts with mainstream music videos that constantly exploit female sexuality.

> ...Speak my mind anytime
> 'Cause I got the master plan...
> I'm a woman on fire with a huge desire
> Gonna be as good as any man...

Capital draws on culture—broken down into signifiers—to frame itself. Cultural allusions that are reduced to stereotypical

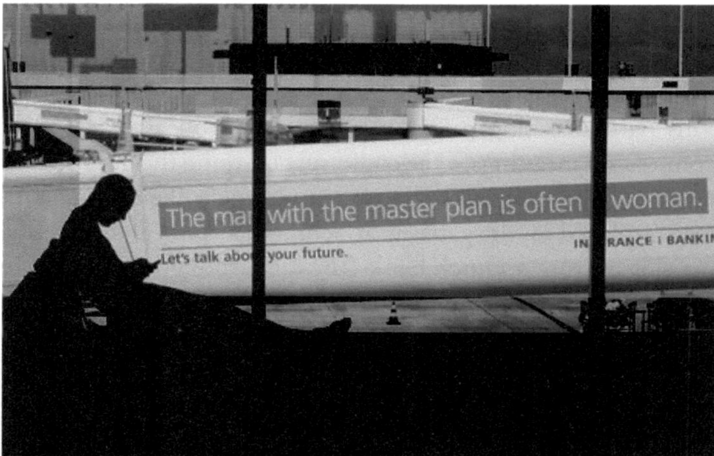

4 Amsterdam Schiphol airport

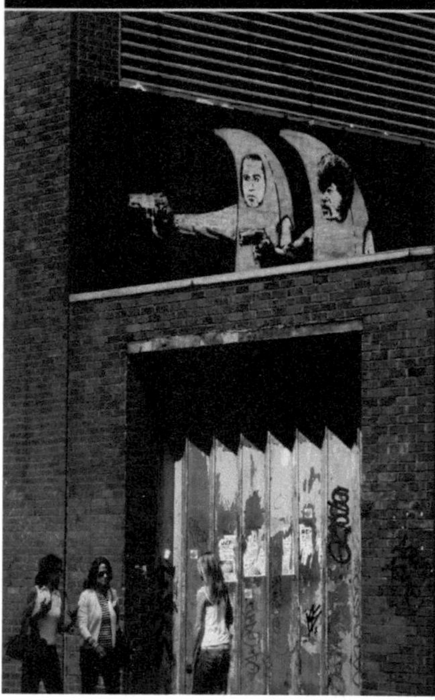

5 Bansky, "Guess who's back"

signifiers provide the constitutive elements used by advertising to signify the impact of globalization caused by neo-liberal economic practices. The global presence of a particular corporation serves as apparent proof that corporate practices are beneficial to all peoples. The amplification of capital as it flows across the globe at an accelerating pace searching for higher rates of return makes use of advertising to legitimize its power as it transforms socio-cultural environments (cf. Klein, 1999). As a consequence, originally subversive works and ideas are themselves appropriated by mainstream media (e.g. http://www.i-shop-therefore-i-am.dk/) and are offered lucrative contracts in return for partaking in 'ironic' promotional campaigns. Slavoj Zizek argues that the kind of distance opened up by cultural jamming (Fig. 5) provides the possibility for ideology to operate:

> ...by attacking and distancing oneself from the sign-systems of capital, the subject creates a fantasy of transgression that "covers up" his/her actual complicity with capitalism as an overarching system. (Slavoj Žižek, 1989)

Floating and pop-up banner ads on the web vividly demonstrate business models on top of still free, accessible information. Equivalent principles thereby play a key role in brand building, i.e. to create an association in the consumer's mind between a recognizable commodity or corporation and imagery of a desirable quality. First and foremost, the brand has to communicate a recognizable but differentiated representation: the logo. That specific representation (the logo or trademark) is attached to a series of layered signifiers that point to a specific set of meanings: the signified. In order to support the branding message it is thus necessary to harmoniously blend layers of audio-visual signifiers so that when we hear the music we think of the slogan. Signifying clusters convey the concept of recurrent and stereotypical clichés drawn from image banks and corporate vaults. Several commercial shots appear pre-coded in that they resemble existing reference systems applied in other media. Hence, the main branding focus is on re-encoding, rearranging and reframing these signifying slices—and the audience should thus complete and decode the signs without much reflexivity.

Baudrillard (1976) attempted to detect an extension of the laws of commodity values to the level of the sign with the aid of a "political economy of the sign." This structural revolution is essentially an attempt to demonstrate how Marx's division of commodity into utility and exchange values was repeated some fifty years later in Saussure's division of the sign into signified and signifier. The replacement of linguistic signs in the circulation of meaning follows the replacement of commodities in the circulation of capital. According to the laws of commodity values, the classical essence of the linguistic is the interchangeability of all signs. We understand the functional dimension of language to include the relationship of the expression to what it signifies, the relationship of the signified to its signifier, just as coin refers to what can be purchased in exchange for it.

Baudrillard argues that the sign is itself a new source of power. We are, he argues, living in a "radical semiurgy", in which production and the commodity have lost their earlier power and given way to the power of signs and simulations. In short the "real" is no longer our benchmark by which to measure our theories and ideas. This is because of this new power of the sign. Baudrillard says we are living in a "hyper-reality".

To understand this position fully it is necessary to note that Baudrillard makes a distinction between on the one hand "dissimulation" and on the other "simulation". The former involves the masking of reality and by implication presupposes/affirms that reality. Simulation is said by Baudrillard to "devour" reality, leaving nothing except signs which merely refer to each other (self-referential). In this sense we are, argues Baudrillard, living in a "virtual reality". The dominance of self-referential signs means that the "real" can itself become the copy of the copy!

In light of future mirror world concepts, ranging from Second Life to the 3D-metaverse, Baudrillard's suggestion that the world we live in has been replaced by a "copy world", where we seek simulated stimuli, has gained new relevance.

As the World Wide Web will soon be absorbed into a "second earth", combining elements of Second Life and Google Earth, the neo-cartographers, -programmers, and -designers of tomorrow will create a map so detailed that it will cover the very things it was designed to represent. It will not be a perfect simulacrum—a hyperreal symbol for something that does not exist, but rather a parallel approach to one's own reality construction. This is a view that underpins my arguments for developing strategies of perception and cognition enabling parallel interpretation models on how we interact in virtual and real worlds. Some of the experiences pertaining to interaction in virtual world scenarios, e.g. in Second Life, indicate several kinds of remediation from the virtual into the real and vice versa. So, for example, companies such as Nike, Toyota, Sun and many others brand their products in a pure virtual fashion, which creates on the other hand considerable real profit. In that respect the symbolic value separates entirely from the commodity value, as the signifier (the trademark) exists solely in a state of virtuality. The real value is generated by the exchange rate for Linden dollars (virtual currency in Second Life) into real currencies. The profitable side effect for companies is thus twofold: a) selling on the one hand pure illusion, and b) seducing the real player in front of the computer screen to purchase the real thing.

In parallel, virtual creations such as avatars and other design products are transformed into real products: 3D printing services for example offer to produce a physical model of an object whose plaster material is built up in layers to form the right shape. Transforming and reformulating existing concepts and representations is essential in the making of (post) modern art, and these are thus being constantly applied and tested in different media-related contexts.

Aside from virtual galleries and replicas already existent in virtual world scenarios, some media artists, e.g. 0100101110101101.ORG[7], confront us with virtual paraphrases of some of the most prominent examples of performance art from the late 1960's and 1970's. These so-called "synthetic performances" (Fig. 6) re-enact the original intention of the performing artists, for example Joseph Beuys' "7000 Oaks" project at Documenta 7 in 1982 in Kassel, Germany. His plan called for the planting of seven thousand trees, each paired with a columnar basalt stone. Even though Beuys' original idea of engaging his art collectors as donors for the project failed, the planting of the last tree in 1987 was made possible through generous foundational support. Beuys intended the Kassel project to be the first stage in an ongoing scheme of tree planting to be extended throughout the world as part of a global mission to effect environmental and social change; locally, the action was a gesture towards urban renewal.

Apparently the socio-cultural transformation process envisaged with the project, the conversion of natural symbols into advanced symbols of creative and ecologically responsible citizenship, has become an attractive pilot for social web move-

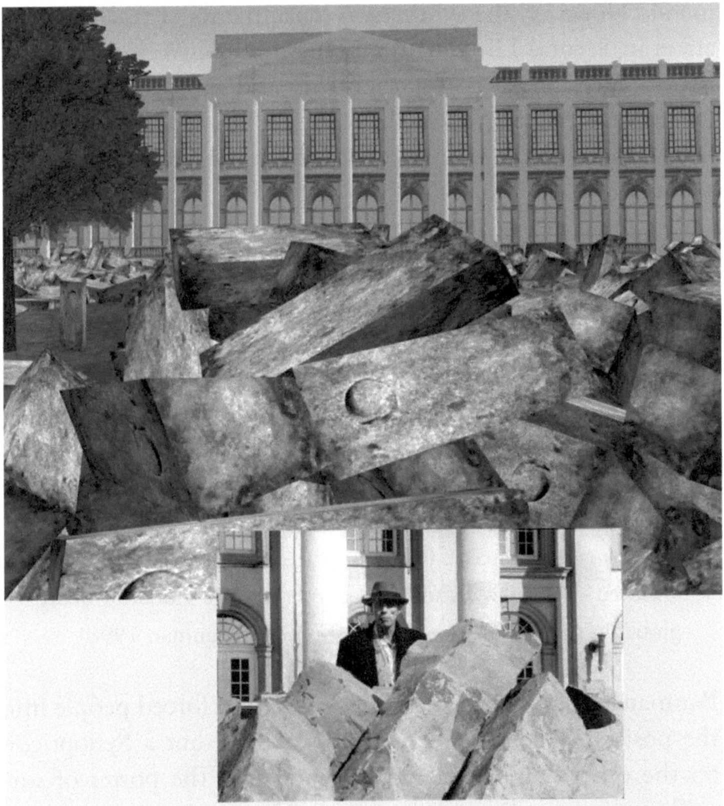

6 Eva and Franco Mattes aka 0100101110101101.ORG, Re-enactment of Joseph Beuys' 7000 Oaks, Synthetic Performance in Second Life, 2007.

ments. However, the synthetic re-enactments of real performances in Second Life blur the boundaries between reality and fiction, fact and fantasy, authenticity and simulation. Thus, it would be interesting to see how the 7000 Oaks project in the form of a synthetic re-enactment will be refashioned again and again…

Ubiquitous Surveillance

> "The many watch the few. The few who are watched are the celebrities. They may come from the world of politics, of sport, of science or show business, or just be celebrated information specialists. Wherever they come from, though, all displayed celebrities put on display the world of celebrities – a world whose main distinctive feature is precisely the quality of being watched – by many, and in all corners of the globe: of being global in their capacity of being watched." (Bauman 1998)

Bauman argues that the Panopticon (Fig. 7) forced people into the position where they could be watched, but a Synopticon on the other hand needs no enforcement. The power of surveillance is spreading among us all. Hence, we constitute the Synopticon by having both the possibility to survey and to be a part of the apparatus. The pervasive power of surveillance emerges through signals, networks and internet connections and they are imaginatively connecting us. Ultimately, we are all part of the game of surveillance, gathered in an electronic arena, where in a fictive menagerie we watch over the selected few. We are covetous of their private life. Their privacy is our required publicity.

Surveillance is a distinctive product of the modern world. Indeed, surveillance helps to constitute the world as modern. Detailed personal information—pursued by many organizations through requests to fill out forms, to produce identification, or to undergo ordeals such as fingerprinting or urine tests—was never routinely and systematically demanded of people before modern bureaucracies came into being. Today, in the so-called advanced societies, people's everyday lives are circumscribed by the record-keeping, monitoring, and supervising of multi-faceted agencies and organizations. Moreover, the ways that personal details are collected, stored, processed, and retrieved depend on rational techniques and increasingly on relatively new technologies. Personal life experiences are shaped, among other things, by relationships with organized social life, and this includes how organizations try to influence, manage, and control us through surveillance.

In pursuit of an overarching convergence culture, technological developments and social processes mutually influence and shape, or co-construct, each other. In order to understand the rapid expansion of surveillance technologies in the latter twentieth century, we need to keep in mind some key characteristics of our postmodern conditions. Whereas the state and the capitalist workplace are the primary sites of surveillance in modern times, computerization has not only augmented surveillance in those sectors but also moved decisively into the consumer sphere. Boundaries between surveillance areas have blurred with regard to surveillance practice, away from past records and present activities to the anticipation and management of future behaviors through data-simulation.

Small- and medium-scale alterations in surveillance practices both reflect broader changes insofar as they form an intrinsic part of daily life today. We blindfoldedly produce passports for

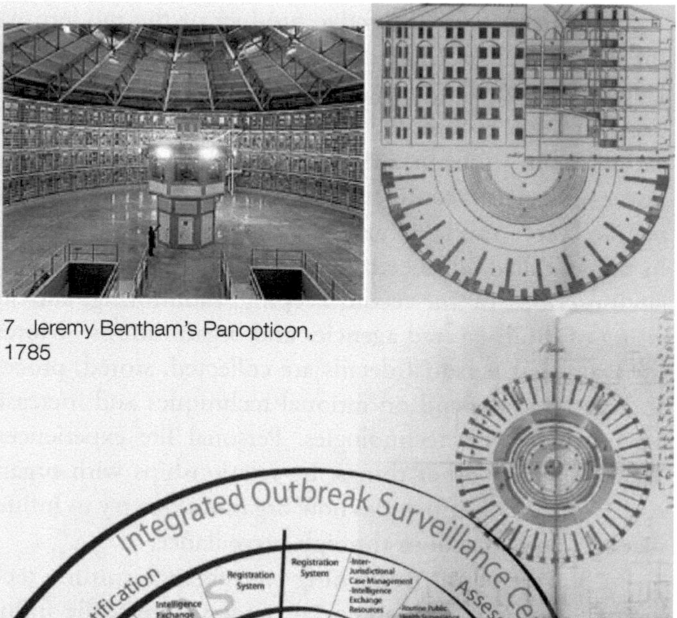

7 Jeremy Bentham's Panopticon, 1785

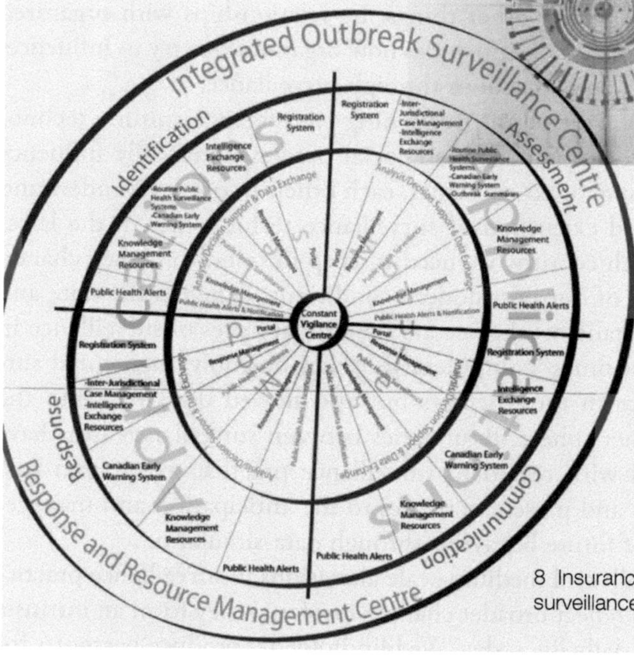

8 Insurance surveillance

scanners to read at airports, feed plastic cards with personal identifiers into bank machines, fill out warranty forms when we buy appliances, key confidential data into telephones or online transactions, drive through automated toll sensors, make cell phone calls, or use bar-coded keys to enter offices or laboratories. How inefficient and inconvenient it would be if we were obliged to pay cash for everything, or to be interviewed by officials each time we cross a border! Nonetheless, at each encounter we leave a trail of personal data that is tracked and processed in ways that impact on our activities and our future life chances.

Surveillance is always Janus-faced and is increasingly seen as the means of obtaining knowledge that would assist in risk management, with the models and strategies of insurance companies taking the lead (Fig. 8). The growth of private security systems is one example of how risk management comes to the fore in stimulating the proliferation of surveillance knowledge.

On the other hand, surveillance itself presents risks, an aspect of what Ulrich Beck (1986) calls the "Risikogesellschaft ("risk society"). Beck has in mind the way that modern industrial production of "goods" seems to carry with it a less obvious production of "bads" in unforeseen side effects and in environmental despoliation. His description of how the risk society arises in autonomized modernization processes which are blind and deaf to their own effects and threats certainly resonates with the expansion of computerized surveillance since the 1960's, even if the risks appear in Orwellian terms. From his perspective, the two faces of surveillance may be thought of as securing against, and unintentionally generating, risks.

At the same time, the scope of insurable or securable risks seems to constantly expand. Prevalent video technologies such as closed circuit television (CCTV) monitor public as well as private spaces. Most if not all of the world's wealthy societies today use surveillance cameras to guard against theft, vandalism or violence in shopping malls, streets, and sport stadiums.

In a BBC news article from 2002 a few of my considerations were addressed regarding the vision of cameras watching your every move:

> The business of surveillance is about to undergo a radical shift as digital cameras become commonplace. Even now, CCTV is the ever-present eye in shopping centres, railway stations and airports and it is most definitely watching you. According to statistics, the average citizen is caught on CCTV cameras 300 times a day. There are 25 million CCTV cameras in operation worldwide, with 2.5 million in the UK.[8]

Biometric methods such as thumbprints or retinal scans may be used to check identities, or genetic tests could be introduced to exclude the potentially diseased or disabled from the labor force. Risks may be managed by aggregating digital data from various kinds of surveillance repositories and techniques for the purpose of collecting and communicating knowledge of risk. Information technologies are also at the heart of another surveillance shift. Not only does surveillance now extend beyond the administrative reach of the state into corporate and especially consumer capitalist spheres, it also extends geographically. Once restricted to the administration of specific territories, surveillance has become a global issue. Globalization and surveillance are thus conjunct by increasing capacities of information technologies that extend the field of surveillance into social and above all commercial relations. The partnerships between major world airlines, for instance, stimulate the global circulation of data. Similarly, the advent of electronic commerce entails huge surveillance consequences.

Especially since the 1990's, then, surveillance has become more intensive and more extensive. Using biometric and genetic methods, it promises to bypass the communicating subject in the quest for identifiable and diagnostic data obtained directly from the body. Through video and CCTV, the optical gaze is reinserted into surveillance practices, which for a while seemed to rely mainly on the metaphor of "watching" to maintain their power. The observable object has turned into a digital data representation, which makes possible optical gaze tracking.

The situation at the turn of the twenty-first century resembles in some respects the surveillance situations of the early twentieth century. The surveillance technology that helped constitute modernity is so to speak an unfinished project. Persons find themselves subject to scrutiny by agencies and organizations interested in influencing, guiding, or even manipulating their daily lives (see Attac). However, the widespread adoption of new technologies for surveillance purposes has rendered that scrutiny discrete and invisible. Physical presence has become less necessary to the maintenance of control, to keeping individuals within a field of influence.

Human-human and human-machine relationships have changed into consumer identities rather than a citizen identity. The most rapidly growing sphere of surveillance is commercial, exceeding the surveillance capacities of most states. Administrative records sought by the state increasingly include those detected from commercial sources—telephone call data, credit card transactions, and so on. This results in "surveillant assemblage" (cf. Haggerty, Ericson 2000) that operates by abstracting human bodies from their territorial settings, and separating them into a series of discrete chunks.These units are then reassembled in different locations as discrete and virtual "data doubles". This surveillant assemblage transforms the purposes and the hierarchies of surveillance, as well as the institution of privacy (ibid.: 1).

Enabled by new technologies, surveillance at the start of the new century is networked, polycentric, and multidimensional, including biometric and video techniques as well as more conventional dataveillance. The same information and communication technologies are the central means of time-space compression, in which relationships are stretched in fresh ways involving remoteness and speed, but are still sustained for particular purposes, including those of influence and control.

Sociospatial Archiving?

Future lifelogs, as envisioned by some of its main protagonists D. Gelernter, G. Bell and S. Mann, will be supplemented through wearable computing, allowing passive continuous voice and visual recording to be augmented with data not directly experienced but held unconsciously as biological "memories", such as physiological conditions inside the body (blood pressure, heart rate, etc.) and external conditions (e.g. orientation, temperature, levels of pollution). Would this "kind of universal prosthetic memory" eradicate immediate perception, as future, past and present wishes, projections and memories blend into each other simultaneously? Does this mean we would retrieve an automatically and nondiscriminatory recorded autobiography, which will be inherently a socio-spatial archive?

Wireless location tracking technologies are already in place and will be further developed into GPS-supported and dynamically collected data so that the precise path of an individual can be recalled. "Subjects" and "objects" can be watched and located anytime, anywhere, e.g. space queries would allow for data retrieval on the location of every personal item within a sensor field, its history, and its relation to other objects, and for recalling every place in which an activity was undertaken.

In his book "When Things Start to Think" (1999), Neil Gershenfeld had already anticipated many of the changes pertaining to pervasive computing, which is premised on the idea of a "memory for life". Although many of these technological promises are equated with human habits of collecting and archiving during their lifetime, the interoperable data exchange between passive and active digital self-surveillance has led to several erroneous conclusions. One of the false assumptions is that this technology can help us to share experiences. If we store memory bits in external databases, we assume that other people can participate in our perception of the world. As there is no unfiltered, objective perception of the world possible, the lifelogger establishes his/her individual context during data capture in comparison with his/her own cognitive and affective map of the world that cannot be executed several times. Consequently, the captured material only provides the external context and excludes the internal context. It is nevertheless the inner world model that permits us to interpret and evaluate the sources based on comparison with existing memory structures.

By nature, the inner context differs among humans, so the differences in interpreting, for example, material collected from a conference would appear rather drastic if one person participated in a plenary session and another did not. Current technology can only turn parts of the human memory outwards, namely, what is called the *episodic memory*, excluding the intellectual and emotional density that affects the memory's quality.

If we want to make an experience transferable, the interplay between episodic and semantic memory (the memory of facts and concepts) must be explicit. If this would ever be technically possible, the attempt of using such knowledge is illusionary because it would take more than a lifetime to analyze it.

The concept of nonforgetting inherent in all lifelog approaches is something that is most feared. Lifelogs, as technologists are seemingly conceiving them, are unforgiving of mistakes because of their ubiquitous and merciless memory. Both forgiveness and amnesty are modifications of collective memory and forgetting, formulating a "universal proposition", so to speak. We thus have to search for another concept, one that is prone to failures and errors.

In search of a fallible lifelog, underpinned by an ethics of forgetting materialized through the inevitable "loss of memory", building fallibility into the system is to ensure a universal aspect of "conditio humana". Lifelogs may never exist without the inclination to breaking rules and norms—which are key sources in creative work. In that sense, I plead for an aesthetic of forgetting, a kind of liberation from history or a rebirth into living in an embodied state in the present moment, the essential ingredient in pervasive computing.

How to Become Invisible

Techniques of surveillance and similarly concepts of counter surveillance privilege the visual aspects, i.e. the questions of representation over the programmable and thus manipulable code which has become the global language in information and network culture. The return of the power of images[9] in almost all socio-relevant contexts marks a new era in how individuals, mass media and electronic networks deal with the technological, aesthetic and social aspects of image production, perception and distribution. One of the strongest arguments justifying the narcissistic bias of watching and being watched in the context of mutual social control accrues from counterstrike techniques opposing "Big Brother's" omnipresent "recording eye". Such techniques, e.g. sousveillance[10], put the individual in the foreground and instead of becoming a targeted victim of the ever-increasing surveillance, he/she is now empowered to play an active role in the production of images, thus creating their own digital repository of images from the perspective of the observer. Different techniques of (self)observation have been proliferating through mass media and web-based communication channels, such as Reality TV shows, mobile imaging and webcams. This tendency of "overexposure" has led to a changing threshold of cultural norms of what is still presentable and acceptable.

It is the interdependency between generous voyeurism and the visibility of offensive exhibitionism that plays an essential role in contemporary media culture. George Berkeley's "Esse est percipii" (to be is to be perceived) contends that individuals can only directly know sensations and ideas of objects; the virtual gaze in contrast creates a closed and an open, a seen and an unseen relationship between subject, object and apparatus. However, the virtual gaze is not only a received perception mediated through representation: it is also encoded "gaze data" fed into networked databases thus being retrievable, manipulable and storable. As a result Esse est percipii converts into esse est 'informatii'.

In the following I will argue that seeming counterstrike techniques such as sousveillance and inverse surveillance, as a situationist critique of surveillance, have less potential to create the envisaged equilibrium between individual and state control. If we look at a famous example from game theory, the "prisoner's dilemma" is a type of non-zero-sum game[11] with two players either cooperating or betraying each other. It is the only concern of each individual player ("prisoner"), as in any other game, to maximize his/her own payoff. In the classic form of this game, cooperating is strictly dominated by "defecting", so that the only possible equilibrium for the game is for all players to defect. No matter what the other player does, one player will always gain a greater payoff by playing defect. Since in any situation playing defect is more beneficial than cooperating, all rational players will play defect, all things being equal.

An example from real life might be helpful to illustrate the idea of a non-zero-sum game: if we consider two cyclists halfway in a race, with the larger group at a great distance behind them, the two cyclists often work together (mutual cooperation) by sharing the load of the front position. If neither of the cyclists makes an effort to stay ahead, the larger group of cyclists will soon catch up (mutual defection). An often-seen scenario is one cyclist doing the hard work alone (cooperating), keeping the two ahead of the crowd so that in the end, the second cyclist (defecting) will likely win because he can ride in the first cyclist's slipstream.

Thus, coming back to the techniques of sousveillance, it appears paradoxical to solve a problem with the same means which actually caused the problem. The assumption of reciprocity-based control in networking culture, which is driven by power laws (e.g. Pareto distribution[12]), conflicts with the hegemonic claims of global capitalism. The mechanisms of control are in fact a non-zero-sum game.

Is there then any counter tactic or strategy that allows the individual to develop appropriate tools to escape from surveillance—and become invisible?

Invisibility is a common theme in tales from science fiction, fantasy, fables and mythology. In H. G. Well's *Invisible Man*, a series of chemical experiments renders a man invisible, yet in practice a chemical approach to invisibility seems rather unlikely. In another fictional invisibility approach, mysterious "fields" are created that can render people and objects undetectable, perhaps by routing the rays of light around the object to be concealed. The Romulans in the Star Trek universe are able to produce fields that can cloak people and other objects, but the energy required to create the fields forms an important limitation to the technology.

When it comes to cloaking, military inventions demonstrate best the intention of becoming invisible, from the early beginning of camouflage up to military cloaking systems such as stealth technology and highly complex metamaterials that cause light or other electromagnetic waves to sweep around the cloak area, to emerge on the other side as if they had passed through an empty volume of space.

It is the bitter irony in the history of human kind that necessity is not the mother of invention, but war. Apparently, we do our best work when we are trying to kill or control each other. Camouflage became an essential part of modern military tactics after the increase in accuracy and rate of fire of weapons at the end of the 19th century. The unexpected effectiveness of submarines led combatant navies to try to confuse the submarines with dazzle camouflage on many ships. This was meant to break up the ship's appearance so that its identity, range and heading could not be easily determined, and the submarine would not be able to achieve a good firing position. A related scheme was the painting of false waves on a ship's bow so that its speed would be overestimated (Fig. 9).

The patterns of military camouflage and its transfer to exclusively civilian uses at the beginning of the First World War also became a symbol of the first industrial war: soon after the German invasion of France in 1914, the couturiers of Paris, who saw the military camouflage on military vehicles, shortly after turned the abstract patterns into women's clothing. In fact, this means that it was used for civilian clothing long before it was used for uniforms.

Scientific and artistic engagement and research with optical illusions at the beginning of the 20th century made visible and explainable through cognitive arguments the phenomenon of eye-deception and the limits of human perception. Further developments in active or adaptive camouflage techniques have thus become the center of military attention, developments which allow an object to blend into its surroundings by use of panels or coatings capable of altering their appearance, color, luminance and reflective properties (Fig. 10). Several examples of almost perfect mimicry can be found in nature, and like the octopus, which can blend into its surroundings by changing skin color as well as skin shape and texture, active camouflage mimics nearby objects as well as objects as distant as the horizon, and the effect should be similar to looking through a pane of glass, making the camouflaged object practically invisible.

The idea of completely making invisible someone wearing a special suit appears in several fictional works; for example in William Gibson's *Neuromancer*, Lupus Yonderboy, the Panther Modern leader, wore a mimetic polycarbon suit made from a fiber that could change colors based on either recorded images or real-time picture input. Other sci-fi technologies such as "thermoptic camouflage" were popularized by Mamoru Oshii's futuristic animated masterpiece, *Ghost in the Shell*.

Apart from fiction, the "invisibility" coat is something of a

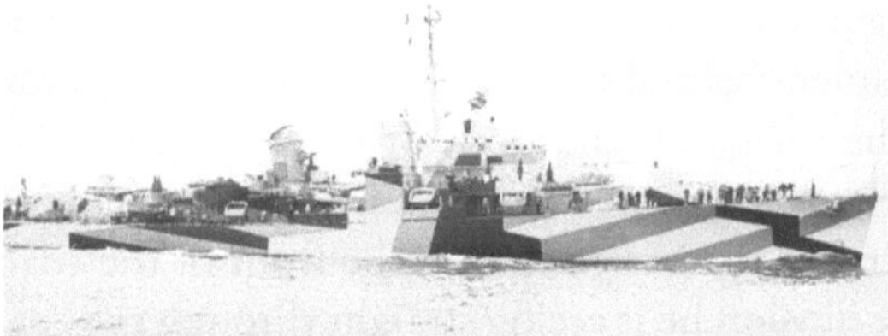

9 Patterns of military ship camouflage

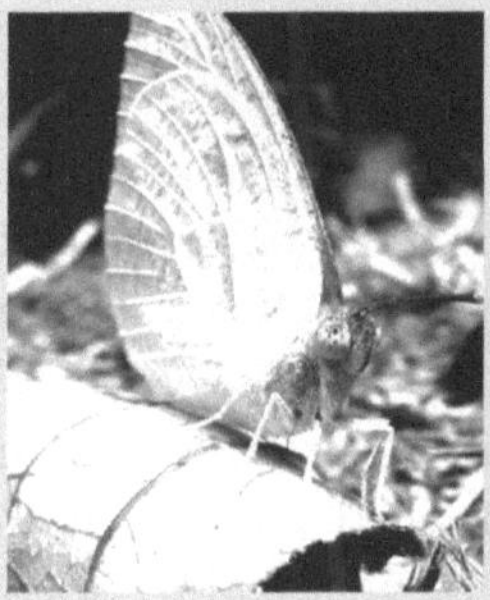

10 Stealth aircraft

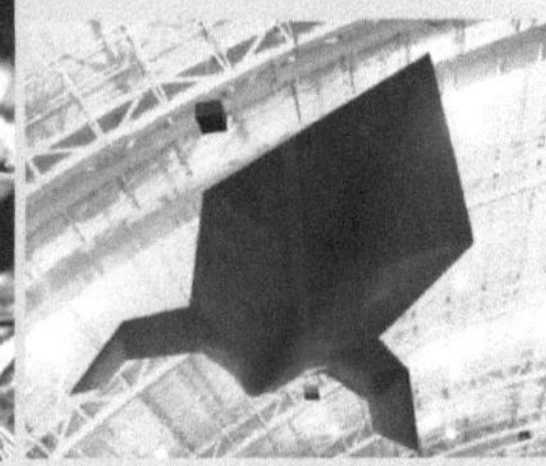

11 Prototype cloaking device of copper rings and wires patterned onto fiberglass sheets

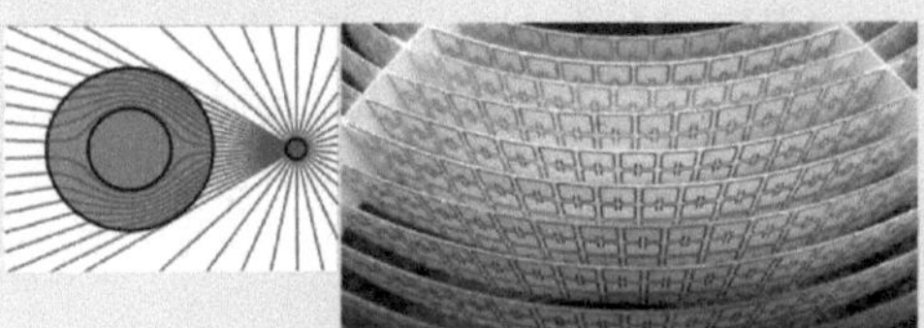

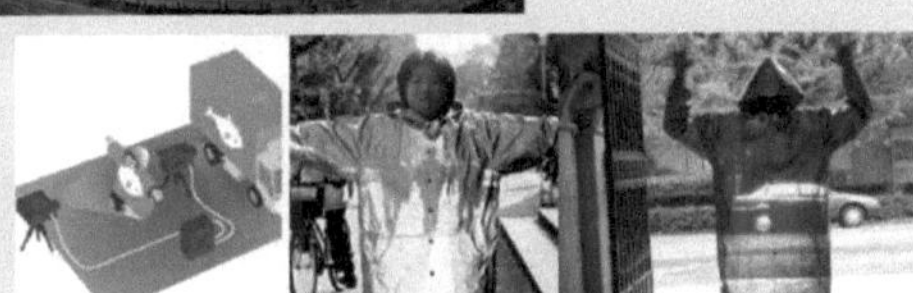

12 Japanese visual stealth jacket

camera trick using microscopic reflectors which act like a movie screen. A video camera behind the coat is linked to a projector, which bounces the image off the front of the coat's reflective surface. Because there is no time lag between what is happening behind the wearer and the image cast on the front of the coat, the viewer has the illusion he is seeing straight through the coat (Fig. 11, 12).

From traditional pattern paintings, to radar-absorbing dark paint, to liquid crystal display and to phased array optics applying a three-dimensional hologram of background scenery, the human race to invent the perfect cloaking device repeats the mythology of Perseus, who went equipped with a helm of invisibility to kill Medusa.

I am using this example from Greek mythology to demonstrate that Perseus applied an early version of augmented reality, insofar as he in parallel had to orientate himself to his surroundings and when slaying Medusa he had to look at her reflection in the mirror instead of directly at her to prevent being turned into stone. This kind of synopsis, the combination of two "realities" by means of human vision and the technical apparatus, together with the magic helm of invisibility, makes Perseus a prototypical example of today's advanced technology-supported warfare tactics.

Becoming invisible in societies of control, with their technologies increasingly reliant on vision surveillance systems, demands strategies other than individual, vision-based strike-back technologies. As visual information becomes digital data fed into distributed databases, any kind of inverse surveillance technique must take up at the level of data manipulation and obliteration. Internet- and biometric-based control techniques mark a new era of post-visual surveillance that turn the mechanism of control and observation into the sphere of electronic communication.

There is no way out of the pictures we create with our recording instruments. Though the record remains fragmented, as there is no recording system available that has the capacity of making a complete documentary of our existence, the current development of human-machine interaction promotes seamless communication, data transfer and retrieval across ubiquitously accessible databases.

Any kind of data feed into global networks like the WWW potentially entails surveillance. The observer is the observed.

4 Blending the Real and the Virtual

Some of the main constraints in computer-mediated information access accrued from the first mainframes up to the desktop computer, which can be characterized as a stable relationship between commodity, technology and user. With the advent of mobile computing technology the user has become increasingly independent from predefined working spaces and technical equipment. Mobile technologies and wireless access points have created a new field of communication and interaction among individuals towards ubiquitous computing. The first trials combining real and virtual world experiences in the late 1960's (e.g. Sutherland's "Head-Mounted Display") opened up a new direction in researching the intro-, extrospective and interactive possibilities with computer technology in light of extending our perceptional apparatus. From the first developments of reality-enhanced concepts through graphics up to the present, a consistent development thread can be drawn including concepts of augmented reality (graphics enhanced by video, reality etc.) and mixed reality, mixing various proportions of virtual and real worlds.

However, virtual reality concepts in which the user interacts with data gloves and head-mounted display have not gained the attention of a broader audience, mainly because of the cut-off from immediate sensation. The so-called total immersiveness best characterizes virtual reality, i.e. the visual, and in some systems aural and proprioceptive senses are under control of the system.

In contrast, augmented reality systems deal with the combination of real world and computer-generated data presupposing that the user maintains a sense of presence in that world.

Virtual images are merged with the real view to create the augmented display.

Azuma[1] (1997) for instance defines an augmented reality system as one that
- combines real and virtual,
- is interactive in real time,
- is registered in 3D.

At present, most AR research is concerned with the use of live video imagery which is digitally processed and "augmented" by the addition of computer-generated graphics. Advanced research includes the use of motion-tracking data, algorithmic marker recognition using machine vision, and the construction of controlled environments containing any number of sensors and actuators.

Mediated reality on the other hand is a term closely related to the experiments with perception by George Stratton at the end of the 19th century. He constructed special eyeglasses ("upside-down glasses") with inverting lenses to demonstrate that one sees a unified world curiously related to one's body. What he wanted to demonstrate is that the unity experienced is not a simple matter of fusing two flat images into a reconstruction of one physical object: it cannot be conceived as a geometrical, physical, or optical model. He concluded that sensual disturbances are neither objective nor subjective as they are not in our cognitive control. They fade as we move around in the world and habituate to our style of engagement with the world. This suggests that the sense of the unity of the visual world and the sense of one's body are meaningful, correlative, labile and habitual. Hence, different styles of looking lag behind changes to our body and its prosthesis; it takes a while to learn how to see the world with new glasses.

A significant attempt to surmount the body-mind dichotomy ("Cartesian Dualism") was Merleau-Ponty's investigation in his Phenomenology of Perception (1945). According to Merleau-Ponty, the human body is an expressive space that contributes to the significance of personal actions. The body is also the origin of expressive movement and a medium for perception of the world. Bodily experience gives perception a meaning beyond that established simply by thought. Thus, Descartes' "cogito ergo sum" does not account for how consciousness is influenced by the spatiality of a person's own body. The primacy of perception signifies a primacy of experience:

> Insofar as I have hands, feet; a body, I sustain around me intentions which are not dependent on my decisions and which affect my surroundings in a way that I do not choose (2002, 440).

Concurrently Merleau-Ponty exemplifies his belief that the body is not restricted by its tangible boundaries where sensorial phenomena occur, i.e. the skin. The corpus may extend itself by rendering external objects as internal and projecting a body-image that is continuously flexible to incorporate new instruments: the blind man's stick has ceased to be an object to him and is no longer perceived as itself; its point has become an area of sensitivity, extending the scope and active radius of touch and providing a parallel to sight (ibid.: 143).

Ironically, virtual reality proponents—most notably Jaron Lanier—suggest new technologies to be partly the "instrument" by which we may override our bodily limitations and reach the transcendental moment. Yet, this instrument is but an extension of the body itself and as such, its whole purpose can only be realized through an embodied experience. This embodiment is, in fact, a spontaneous prerequisite for communicating in virtual environments and interacting with the interface, which is by no means a pure mental construct but an innumerable amount of sensory dialogues (seeing, hearing, touching, etc). As the body is the basis for our interactions and perceptions, virtual space can only be seen as a symbiotic synthesis of technology and corporeal phenomena.

Hence, virtual tools cease to be external objects and become part of human body and mind, just as the blind man's stick becomes an extension of his sensorial activity. As a consequence, the construction of self in virtual environments follows an alternative mode of "representation", which synergizes the physical and the virtual: the mind and body become one in order to pursue a unified goal, and if either is missing, the result is the non-existence of the experience. Roughly speaking, in virtual environments one is, in effect, embodied in one's disembodiment. In sharp contrast to "Prosthetics, Robotics & Remote Existence"[2] by the Australian artist Stelarc, the body in this context is no longer seen as the obsolete object or the inert container of the mind, but an integral entity reassigned with the indispensable role of the medium.

An interesting experiment from the latest research in cognitive neuroscience underpins the previous arguments that our perceptions of 'self' are confined to our own bodies. But what exactly is 'self'? Two groups of scientists have taken steps to answering these questions using illusion and deception.

One of the first experiments scientists conducted were recordings of the human brain's awareness of its own body, using the illusion of a strategically-placed rubber hand to trick the brain. Their findings provided information about disorders of self-perception such as schizophrenia, stroke and phantom limb syndrome, where sufferers may no longer recognize their own limbs or may experience pain from missing ones (Fig. 1).[3]

By manipulating volunteers' perceptions of their own body via three different senses—vision, touch and proprioception—they found that one area of the brain, the premotor cortex, integrates information from these different senses to recognize the body. However, because vision tends to dominate, if information from the senses is inconsistent, the brain "believes" the visual information over the proprioceptive. Thus, someone immersed in an illusion would feel, for example, that a fake limb was part of their own body.

Another experiment focused on inducement of out-of-body experiences in healthy volunteers, by using virtual reality headsets to deceive reagents by projecting themselves into a virtual body. Volunteers watched their own backs as filmed by a camera behind them and projected in front of them with a video headset. Their backs were then stroked with a highlighter at the same time as the virtual body's (Fig. 2).[4] In response to the sensation the volunteers felt, they reported that it seemed to be caused by the highlighter stroking their virtual back rater than their real back. They felt as if the virtual body was their own, in the same way that people fall for the rubber hand illusion.

Some of the conclusions drawn from both studies reveal new findings on how our brains generate a sense of self: they compile our usual 'in-body' experiences by amalgamating information from our senses, including, at the very least, sight and touch. The research demonstrates that our brains will choose interpretations that fit with the information from these senses, and apparently, vision is most important. It can override and modify the information from touch. Consequently, virtual reality illusions can be used to work out how this area contributes to our self-consciousness.

The "return to illusions" as a suggestive postulate, last but

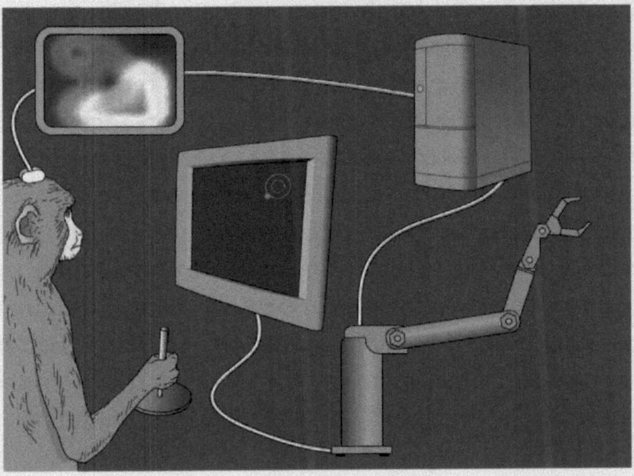

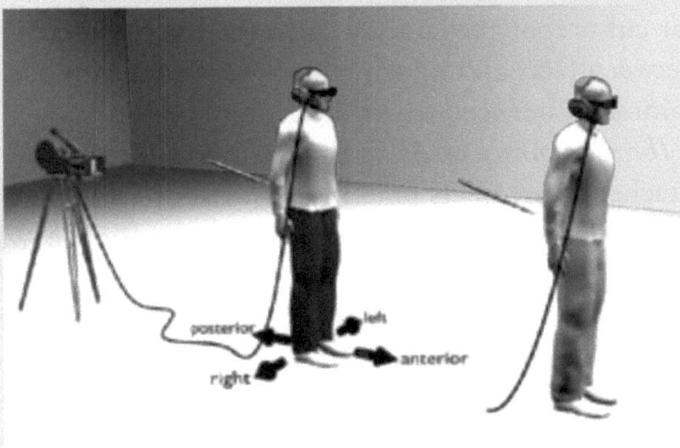

1 Monkey's brain signals control 'third arm'
2 Inducement of out-of-body experiences

not least triggered by cognitive neuroscience, may accommodate Baudrillard's wishful thinking to return back to appearance in the world of illusions rather than disappearing in the world of simulations. However, he states that with the most advanced technologies we may find a way back to a radical condition of illusion. A necessary prerequisite for this illusionary state of perception is the distinction between the "real" space and the representation of space. Accordingly, the subject embodies universality and the object singularity. If one of these entities diminishes or even collapses our perception and judgment becomes indifferent and thus meaningless. Therefore Baudrillard uses the concept of simulation, which refers to the creation of the real through conceptual or "mythological" models that have no connection or origin in reality. In this case the model becomes the determinant of our perception of reality—the real. Popular culture, or the cultural industry, has blurred the frontiers between facts and information, between information and entertainment, between entertainment and politics.

In *The Conspiracy of Art*[5], Baudrillard questions the privilege attached to art by its practitioners. Baudrillard holds Marcel Duchamp and his ready-mades (e.g. "The Bicycle Wheel", 1913 and "Fountain", 1917) responsible for an overarching aesthetization of everything: "Art is everywhere but in art." He calls for an autonomous art lifted and separated from "value," from obscene "proximity" to the viewer, from the interactivity where "you" (the viewer) are the artist. Yet, the *YOUniverse* as it appears in social web developments suggests rather the contrary: the privileged status of the artist, author as the single creator and originator of the artwork, is now confronted with the "vox populi" of network culture and its rhizome-like hybrid forms of interaction between humans and artificial agents. The appearance of this novel movement represents a revolutionary cultural achievement inasmuch as the tools of media creation and critique are put in the hands of citizens themselves. From the vantage point of media evolution, beginning with one-to-one (telephone), to one-to-many (TV, radio) up to many-to-many communication (Web), it appears enticing at first glance to generally speak about a tendency towards democratization of media. Verifiably mass media, television in particular, conveys the opposite. For example, the number of corporations that control a majority of U.S. media shrank from 50 in 1983 to 5 major players in 2004: Time Warner, Disney, Murdoch's News Corporation, Bertelsmann of Germany, and Viacom (formerly CBS).[6]

> The major media are large corporations, owned by and interlinked with even larger conglomerates. Like other corporations, they sell a product to a market. The market is advertisers - that is, other businesses. The product is audiences, [and] for the elite media, [they are] relatively privileged audiences. So we have major corporations selling fairly wealthy and privileged audiences to other businesses. Not surprisingly, the picture of the world presented reflects the narrow and biased interests and values of the sellers, the buyers and the product.
> Noam Chomsky (from Take the Rich Off Welfare)

With regard to diversification of the media landscape we can ascribe to the authentic and participatory media approach of the blogosphere attributes such as immediacy, originality, spontaneity, and disruptiveness on its way back to "the real", whereas mass media in contrast pursues to entertain, deceive and manipulate its audience. Behind this logic operates the consumption function of information, meaning the major flows of information produced for and disseminated by TV, radio, by books, magazines and newspapers, are appropriated for consumption only. This has nothing to do with the real world, with the decision-making processes or any other requirements of the users, except the consumption itself. Juvenal's "Panem et Circenses" (Bread and Circuses) implies that the masses have staved off democracy and substituted spectacles that narcotize the public via mass entertainments. The entertainment business operates substantially through the mechanism of the illusory world: the violence on television, real and fictional, merges; the fictional becomes real to us, while the real becomes fictional. Or speaking with McLuhan, the more a medium shows, the "cooler" it becomes because there is less work for the mind to do. In contrast, a "hot" medium in McLuhanian terms demands completion by a participant who engages in personalized media, which would suggest a new era of media reception and perception. However, the (ME)edia turnaround some of the main proponents of personalized mass media (P. Saffo[7]) have in mind does in fact not advance to change the power structure of mass media; rather, it imposes upon users to organize the voluminous media bombardments themselves.

Metaverse Interplays and Collisions

Before dealing with the augmentative, intimate, external and simulative aspects of interconnected metaverse scenarios, it appears helpful to revive some of the core concepts of everyday practices and to connect these with the complex spatio-temporal, socio-cultural and techno-aesthetic implications of ubiquitous computing.

Michel de Certeau (1984), one of the most influential theorists of "the everyday", brought into discussion the ways in which people individualize mass culture, altering things from utilitarian objects to street plans to rituals, laws and language, in order to make them their own. The utility and potential of digital technologies had not yet emerged and is therefore not present in de Certeau's work, yet his models of strategies and tactics put the "user" in the foreground. The concept of "consumption" is expanded in the phrase "procedures of consumption" which then further transforms to the "tactics of consumption" that became seminal in the emerging realms of digital cultural production and participation.

In 1991, Mark Weiser, who coined the term ubiquitous computing already in 1988, wrote in his groundbreaking Scientific American article, "The most profound technologies are those that disappear. They weave themselves into the fabric of everyday life until they are indistinguishable from it." ("The Computer for the 21st Century") In other words, the social-driven approach of the so-called calm technologies privileges the invisible tool that does not intrude on our consciousness but keeps us focused on the task, like eyeglasses: you look at the world, not the eyeglasses.[8]

In a way, Weiser was convinced that not only would ubiquitous computing liberate us from the constraints of desktop computing, but more importantly it would free us from equally isolating immersive and simulated virtual reality environments. Weiser's fundamental critique of Virtual Reality originated from a time when VR represented a unique mix of military, university and counter-culture values. In sharp contrast to the seemingly boundless freedom promised by the main VR proponents at that time, Ubicomp (Ubiquitous computing) did not aspire to transcend real world experiences but rather "…to make technology conform to the needs of people" (Norman, 1998:261).

Bringing the socially cohesive technology approach of Ubicomp to an understanding of everyday life means that notions of performative practice, embodied interaction and contextualization need to be more deeply investigated. With the advent of ambient intelligence, the larger scale socio-economic and socio-political dimensions of context have become more explicit (e.g. e-health, e-government) in contrast with the focus on the smaller scale anthropological study of social (mainly workplace and private ambience) practices inherent in the concept of ubiquitous computing.[9]

To develop further understanding of performative practice and socio-technical multitudes, in the context of the design and evaluation of ubiquitous computing and ambient intelligence, we need to consider the technical and the social sphere in which embodied interactions can unfold. In this regard we owe to Garfinkel's ethnomethodology[10] a helpful orientation regarding the orderliness of social conduct—what he calls "the documentary method"—where people can contextualize and interpret meaningfully their everyday actions. Accordingly, the meaning of technology is not inherent in the technology but arises from how technology is used. Apparently the meaningful use of everyday technology requires contextual and organizational as much as spatial/physical skills and competences in shaping action and in providing people with the means to interpret and understand action. Whether it concerns human-human or human-machine communication, meaning of action accrues from interaction. Temporal context is also involved insofar as novel forms of expressions and strategies of encoding and decoding multimodal information (e.g. chatting, teleporting, short messaging) gain their meaning and intelligibility from being interpreted as part of a larger pattern of activities. This suggests that the meaning of the use of technology is in permanent flux and thus prone to readjustments in order to be able to support the communication of meaning through it, within a community of practice.

Ambient intelligent environments are characterized by inter-related bio-physical and psycho-dynamic dimensions of bodies, individually and collectively, in specific spatio-temporal contexts whereas virtual world encounters, for example in Second Life, confine us to our desktop and most of the time constrain our bodily abilities to poor sitting postures.

In the following, I will bring into the discussion some of the current and future metaverse scenarios with specific regard to the intersubjective ways in which individuals manage social and cultural material within the context of switching between real and virtual encounters in everyday life, involving a move from conventional totalizing perspectives to micrological approaches. This less deterministic and schematic view is more aware of the constitutive contradictions that characterize and structure the entire issue.

Personal Spaces

With the notion of space many people spontaneously make associations with their immediate surroundings. This so-called personal space is the region surrounding each person or that area we think of as something that belongs solely to ourselves.

In his social interactive artwork Boundary Functions (1998) Scott Snibbe demonstrates that personal space exists only in relation to others, and it changes dynamically in relation to those around us.[11] The underlying theory behind his artistic concept derives from mathematics, the Voronoi diagram, named after Russian mathematician Georgy Voronoi. In principle, a Voronoi diagram is a collection of regions that divide up a plane. Each region corresponds to one of the sites, and all the points in one region are closer to the corresponding site than to any other site. These diagrams are applied in several fields to describe, for example in anthropology and geography, patterns of human settlement; in biology, the patterns of animal dominance and plant competition; in astronomy the influence of gravity on stars and star clusters; in marketing the strategic placement of chain stores; in robotics path planning; and in computer science the solution to closest-point and triangulation problems.[12] Exemplarily, Snibbe's Installation concept sketch demonstrates that if more than two people are on stage, the floor becomes divided into cellular regions, each with the mathematical quality that all space within the region is closer to the person inside than any other (Fig. 3).

Another concept looking at personal spaces refers to *proxemics*, a term coined by anthropologist Edward T. Hall in 1959 to describe measurable distances between people as they interact. According to Hall, body spacing and posture are unintentional reactions to sensory fluctuations or shifts such as subtle changes in the sound and pitch of a person's voice. He also discovered that social distance between people correlates with physical distances categorized by Hall as measurable delineations of intimate, personal, social and public distance (Fig. 4).[13]

The appeal "don't stand so close to me" goes hand in hand with the so-called "elevator effect". A recent study conducted by NPR found that misbehavior creates the same discomfort no matter whether it happens in real or in virtual life. Thus, it is no surprise that Hall's observations and research of nonverbal communication or proxemic behavior categories gain fresh momentum in virtual societies (Fig. 5).

By the end of 2008, half of the world's 6.7 billion people will live in urban areas, according to a recent report by the United Nations. As the space around us becomes denser, people with wealth will search for new ways to separate themselves from the masses. Therefore interest in the issue of personal space—that invisible force field around your body—is intensifying in both real and virtual world contexts. Based on research evidence[14], some avatars' physical behavior in Second Life conforms with unspoken behavioral rules of humans, for example, on how to protect their personal space, even though they are but pixels on a screen. It was also observed that both humans and their digital representations tend to avert eye gaze if they feel someone is standing too close. They retreat to corners, put distance between themselves and strangers, and sit or stand equidistant from one another whereas men keep more space between each other than women. What the study therefore specifically found is that unwritten rules of personal space are so powerful, people even impose them on their cyberselves. It would go beyond the scope of this book to more closely focus on individual space behaviors and their embodiments in virtual worlds. However, what can be concluded from actual research findings suggests that a major part of virtual world inhabitants feel physiologically uncomfortable about breaking the rules, social norms and real-life stereotypes. Human nature may be the same no matter what brand new world we discover.

Another important aspect relates to interferences and disturbances caused by intervention in public and private spaces with mobile technologies. We are acting in the public sphere, handling private or professional phone calls, and simultane-

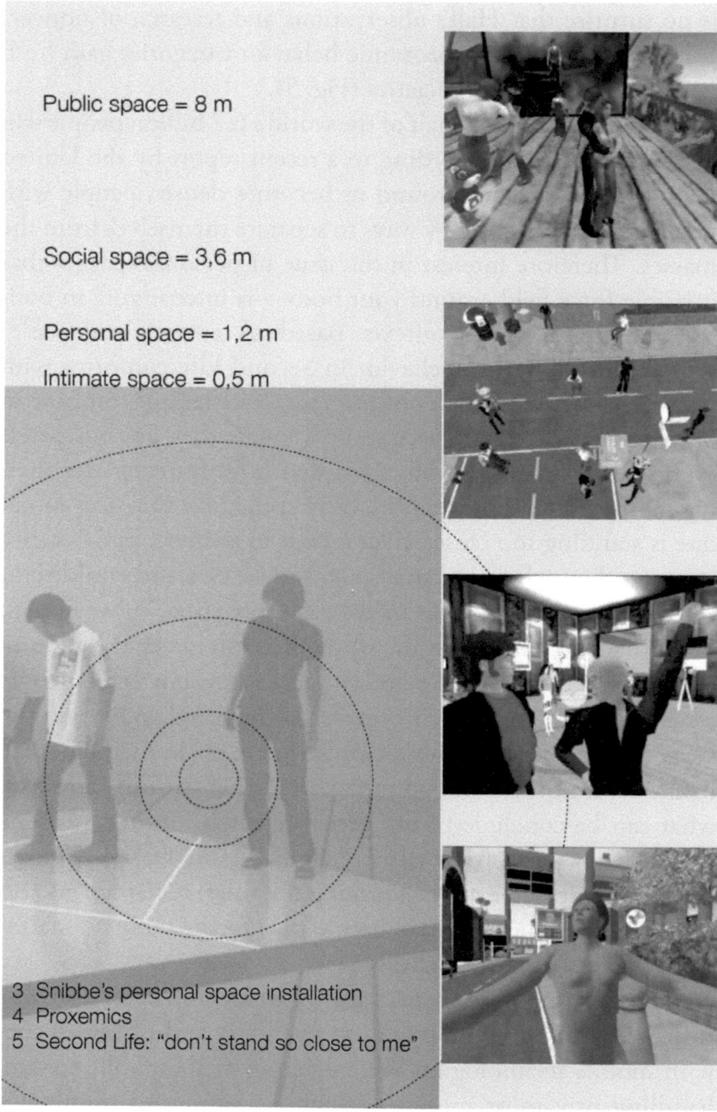

3 Snibbe's personal space installation
4 Proxemics
5 Second Life: "don't stand so close to me"

ously entering a set of personal and electronic networks. We also experience that the borders between institutional settings, social systems, individual roles and intersubjective relationships are becoming a) more permeable, insofar as components of one sphere can more easily enter the other; b) more flexible to the degree that the extension of different spheres can be varied according to current situations and needs; and c) more interpenetrating (or "blending"), insofar as role activities may expand and belong to different domains at the same time (Geisler et. al. 2001).

A practical example might be useful to understand how 3D simulations and the real world will be overlapping and locally accessible through location-aware mobile devices such as wireless phones. A GPS-enabled camera phone could serve as a temporary window into the Metaverse and combined with social media, place becomes a powerful way to communicate. Imagine walking past a city location (a museum or a bar, for instance) and pulling out your mobile device to see which of your friends have been there before, and also if anyone has written any reviews. Or you could even annotate specific locations with virtual world models, photographs, or music. Each photograph taken at a certain spot and time becomes geospatially tagged (this allows you to put your photographs on the world map in the exact spot they were taken) as conversation thread for that location.

We do not yet know how the extension of physical space will affect individual and collective behavioral patterns in either modes of switching between real and virtual identities, augmenting sensory perception of real-life objects with retinal projected images, or being entirely immersed in 3D data spaces.

Will the immediate individual physical space, determined by imagined boundaries, and the mediated space become an intertwined yet indistinguishable illusionary trick of being in the world of simulation and appearance at the same time? What does the framework for a massive virtual economic and social space look like? And who will control the future "myspaces"?

Spatial Orientation and Navigation

We acquire spatial knowledge through direct environmental exposure by means of selective extraction of information and a number of secondary sources such as maps, photographs, videotape, and recently virtual environments. But how do we store and organize spatial knowledge in the mind for future application? The psychological transformations by which an individual can acquire, code, store, recall, and decode information about the relative locations and attributes of phenomena in their everyday or metaphorical spatial environment is generally known as a cognitive map.[15] Cognitive maps are in fact a method we use to structure and store conscious perceptions, but also automatic (subconscious) encodings of spatial relations to help determine our current position, where specific objects are in surrounding space, and how to get from one place to another (Fig. 6).

The representation of spatial knowledge is affected by the method used to acquire it. Knowledge gained from direct navigation differs from knowledge acquired from a paper map, or an audiovisual or interactive computer map on the screen. We know from experience the confusion between the mental representation of a specific location gained from a map and what is actually being seen. For example, if we read our city map with north at the top of the map and then enter the city by car from the north, this requires a 180° mental rotation before the cognitive map can be in line with the real environment (Fig. 7). Spatial knowledge acquired from maps tends to be orientation specific. The map can be thus either used as a tool to precede or to be concurrent with navigation. If maps are used concurrently with navigation, the placement of oneself is necessary on the map. "Where am I? What direction am I facing?" as common questions indicate the required transformation from an egocentric perspective to an exocentric perspective, which in our case represents geospatial data. There is no transformation required if a map is used only for planning and familiarization. Difficulties mostly occur when a perspective transformation must be performed so that the rotation of the map can have a great effect on performance. Research evidence[16] suggests that maps used during navigation tasks (egocentric tasks) should be oriented "forward-up" (the top of the map shows the environment in front of the viewer) while maps used for planning or other geocentric tasks should be "north-up".

In current mobile map-application developments[17] we can see how automated positioning, rotating of maps and intuitive gesture control for zooming and scrolling facilitates navigation. Some of the features include positioning and rotating according to current location and orientation with context-sensitiveness and gesture control. Depending on where we are locatable "in situ" by means of geospatial positioning (GPS) and other trace-back mechanisms, specific communication processes can be triggered either through participatory media involvement or service-based information retrieval.

The way we navigate, orientate and communicate in real and virtual surroundings becomes increasingly context dependent in ambient intelligent environments. Smart car developments for example have long since caught up with science fiction (e.g. the Tribal Pizza Carputer in Neil Stephenson's Snow Crash) by using advanced communication systems including computers, wireless networking and GPS. As individual traffic increases exponentially, intelligent cars might be a solution to interactively ease traffic congestion and take more favorable routes as traffic needs arise. From the point of view of engineers smart cars will also be intelligent enough to avoid pedestrians, cyclists and others not driving automobiles.

Will this mean a radical suspension or demise of our innate sensual abilities in the future? Or do all these developments point to the union of human and machine, in which the knowledge and skills embedded in our brains will be combined with the vastly greater capacity, speed, and knowledge-sharing ability of our own creations? This is by far the most radical futurist perspective and—understandably—also the most contentiously debated era of human nature and evolution: the technological creation of smarter-than-human intelligence.[18] The reason I am referring to *Technological Singularity* is the admittedly positivistic vision of the ostensible predictability of human evolution, which is solely based on the assumption that technical improvement creates superhuman intelligences being capable of better surviving on this planet. A rather different approach that brings us back to human evolution relates to the concept of *Consciousness Singularity*[19], which refers to a hypothetical point of time in the future when human consciousness, at both the personal and species level, experiences an abrupt transition into a collective state of transcendence, a state that is conceptually impossible for us to imagine "what it's like" with our current limited cognitive abilities.

How deceptive our brain truly is in terms of visual perception and interpretation has been recently discovered by scientists at UCL (University College London). They have found the link between what we expect to see and what our brain tells

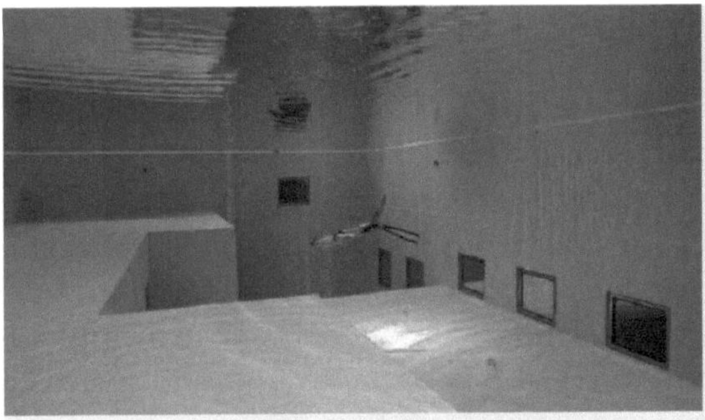

6 Spatial immersion, relationship and context

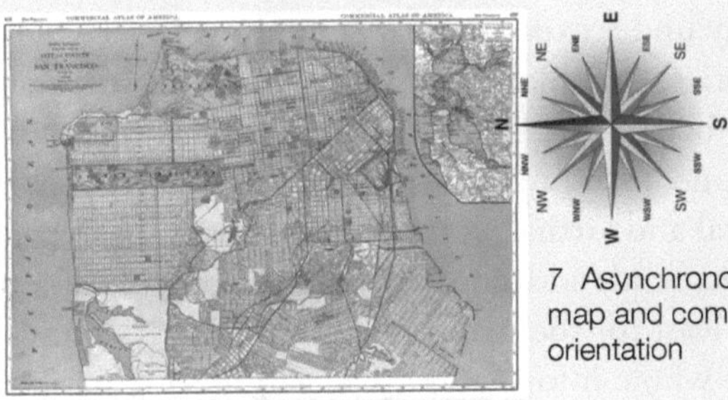

7 Asynchronous map and compass orientation

8 Convergence of Second Life and Google Earth

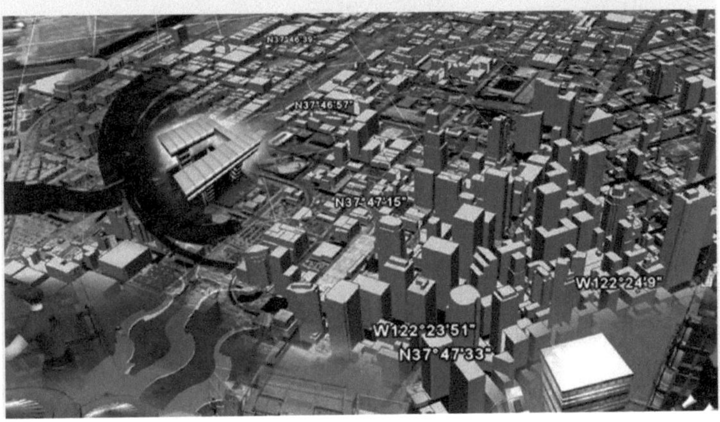

us we actually saw. The study reveals that the context surrounding what we see is all important—sometimes overriding the evidence gathered by our eyes and even causing us to imagine things that are not actually there.[20]

Thus our spatial ability is context dependent, meaning the perception of our environment through our senses, the cognitive process of how we learn about our environment and the relationships between objects, needs to be permanently adjusted to our peripheral perceptions, motivation and strategies. Spatial and navigational awareness thus proves to be reliable especially under experimental conditions (zero gravity in space laboratories) in which both procedural and survey knowledge needs to be applied.

Yet, one of the major obstacles to seamlessly switching between real and virtual world environments is the current interface. It demands additional skills and a considerable amount of time (at least for the major pragmatists) to become acquainted with the whole information, navigation, orientation and creation features in Second Life. Once you have teleported yourself via a "world map" to a specific spot on the map, the abruptness of being represented in an interactive virtual environment usually clashes with the spontaneity and intuitiveness of daily routine. Starting as an avatar novice, the collision between real world movements and gestures becomes even more apparent as the tools for navigation and interaction need to be rehearsed and applied to certain tasks, such as finding and creating things (geolocations, info repositories, buildings, applications) and interacting with people (meetings, presentations etc.).

The process of wayfinding, which means in real world terms the ability to accurately relocate from one place to another in a large-scale space, can be similarly applied to constructing aids (environmental cues, landmarks) for wayfinding in virtual

worlds. Such tools and mediators need to fulfill certain criteria with regard to:
a) Map usage (e.g., the user's position and view direction on the map needs to be updated dynamically);
b) Landmarks (e.g., users should be allowed to annotate the environment by means of personalized spatial cues, which are easily adaptable to a wide variety of navigation tasks);
c) Trails of footprints (e.g., users may use them appropriately in the context of a specific exhaustive search but should turn them off afterwards);
d) Directional cues (e.g., users can effectively use them when moded and used with directional landmarks since directional cues place landmarks in a global coordinate system).

Environmental learning and development follow a series of differing information processing systems, rather than one general mechanism. Originally it was assumed that the learning process follows a linear structure of subsequent stages from landmark knowledge to route knowledge and finally to survey or configurational knowledge. Other studies[21] showed that route knowledge can be acquired prior to landmark knowledge or even without landmarks at all. In fact, some research has suggested that survey knowledge can already be acquired during the initial period of an environmental learning task. Current spatial cognition research deals with questions on how these processes interact or can be altered under different conditions. If, for example, a person deals with a mapping task to collect information simultaneously about an environment, the acquisition of configurational knowledge, such as metric distances and cardinal directions, becomes simplified. A wayfinding task containing environmental information can be approached only iteratively through travel and memorization of sequential route directions and landmarks.

In conclusion, environmental competencies involve two different information processing systems (simultaneously and sequentially) and two different strategies in environmental learning (configurational and route strategy). Route instructions in a descriptive manner are less precise and are thus prone to ambiguity. For some people it may suffice to acquire information by landmark descriptions such as "go to the big church" or by adding relational directions such as "turn right at the next traffic light". Others may only use route directions such as "go straight ahead, second turn left".

Configurational knowledge[22] in its fully-developed form would allow a person to estimate absolute distances and directions between known points corresponding with a geometrically-correct map. However, the variety in quantity and quality of competencies in wayfinding and environmental knowledge may help explain individual preferences for one strategy over another.

In the future metaverse, where real environments, individuals and groups will be able to seamlessly communicate and interact with virtual environments, avatars and intelligent "bots", mobile assistance systems are likely to become indispensable for navigation in the car, digital guidance for pedestrians and handicapped people, mobile workers collecting on-the-spot data and many more. Thereby the configurations of available services, networks, and other infrastructure components will constantly change, depending on the respective locations and situations. Intelligent software systems including position technologies such as Global Positioning System (GPS), GSM positioning, Wireless LAN positioning or Bluetooth positioning keeps track of where the user is located in space. By entering and uploading information, the system automatically allocates a latitude-longitude coordinate. In this way, location-based information systems create user experiences similar to those of post-its, graffiti and public signs and posters.

Bridging physical and virtual world interactions in an unobtrusive and seamless way requires not only an interplay of intelligent artifacts and complex information systems corresponding to mixed real/virtual settings, but also the mental and physical dispositions of human beings to deal with augmented world views (Fig. 8).

Some of these new user interface scenarios contain:

a) Teleport hubs that channel visitors through a designed path; a welcome center; street names; robot guides; and more;

b) Active contact lenses that would allow you to see the real and virtual world, or a mixture of the two. For example, you may enter a meeting room and receive a call from someone in the virtual world; you instantaneously switch into a mixed reality mode, instead of talking on your mobile phone;

c) Networked homes with embedded sensors that capture speech, movements and odors, so that you could remotely step into your own virtual home world;

d) Multi-channel communication that stimulates role-playing skills and cross-cultural understanding within globally connected environments;

e) Internet bots that collect, store and process information for you. You could for example instruct your avatar to walk around the world searching for like-minded communities, so when you are next online there are a whole host of interesting people for you to meet.

As many-worlds encounters become more commonplace, we are likely to adjust to them as communication spaces that will perhaps encourage new kinds of creativity. However, the person on the street gesticulating with an 'invisible real' but 'visible virtual' counterpart holds a variety of unforeseen surprises—a perhaps abrupt and hard landing.

Communication, Participation, Exploitation

Virtual spaces allow many people from around the world to meet, talk and collaboratively work together from their home or any other connected environment. Telephone conferences were one of the first attempts to achieve a shared communicative space in which individuals were able to sequentially talk to many people at the same time. The dialogical principle of a discussion taking place in real space was consequently transferred into a verbally mediated telematic space. In telecommunication, the modality of information and communication stays rather confined to hearing whilst the other senses of touch, smell, sight, and taste are excluded, or at least not perceivable for the non-present vis-à-vis. From a historical point of view, telephony was an intimate and locally based means of communication until mobile devices made it public. One could also argue that a certain intimacy adhered to telephone conversations (except for anonymous wiretapping and disturbances) whereas mobile technology recaptured the public domain, yet in a different manner from the classical place of assembly, the Greek agora. With mobile communication technology phoning we intrude into the public and individual sphere twofold: as a wired, verbal and emotional-expressive protagonist and as an encapsulated, non-communicative entity amidst complex relationships. Apart from cumulative adoption of ubiquitous connectivity, behavioral norms, social structures and forms of interaction can hardly keep pace with the rapidity of technological progress. It seems that the wish for nearness and the desire for simultaneous messaging ("I want you to be next to me") by means of communication technologies bears a certain kind of paradox: we often develop relationships with what is far at the expense of what is immediately around us. Without doubt, technology bridges the gap between long distances and facilitates communication, but at the same time, people become alienated within the proximity.

The advent of modern communication technologies brought about the death of distance. This means that a sudden remoteness of objects is no constraint to accessing them in some mediated way. Consequently, this new ordering of distance acts not only upon what is far, but also what is near. The seeming collapse of the Euclidian metric of space and time, the move from mass communication to interactive digital media—what Pierre Levy (1998) refers to as virtualization, suggests a different mode of cultural representation instead of mere technological change. Speaking in Paul Virilio's (1997) terms the shift from chronological (relative speed of geographic transport) to chronoscopic (speed-of-light transmission) time marks the shift to an instantaneous mode of production and consumption.

Approaching the nearness-distance dichotomy from an epistemological point of view, the object, the other, can be quite far from us even when it is physically near, and similarly things that are physically far can be epistemologically near. Referring to this notion, Paul Freire suggests the term epistemological distance as a method that allows us not to directly focus our attention on the object challenging us in the process of knowledge discovery.

Instead of taking the object in hand to get to know it, he proposes an "epistemological encircling" (Freire 1997: 92), in the sense that the interior of the object is apprehended in relationship with others. In other words, the Aristotelian conception of objects that remain of constant nature, no matter the context in which the object is put, pursues the concept of substantialism and authoritarianism, whereas the concept of relationalism refers to dialogical principles and democratic institutions.[23]

> "There is no communication without dialogism, and communication lies at the core of the vital phenomenon. In this sense, communication is life and a vector for more-life. But, if communication and information occur on the level of life upon its support, let us imagine its importance and, thus, that of dialogism for human existence in the world. On this level, communication and information are served by sophisticated languages and by technological instruments that "shorten" space and time. The social production of language and of instruments with which human beings can better interfere in the world announce what technology will be." (Dewey 1966: 92 ff)

Freire undoubtedly owes much to Mikhail Bakhtin's Dialogism, a concept that stresses the bond of questions and responses, situated in a sphere where relations are relations of meaning that express themselves through language and signs but are not reducible to these two dimensions. A dialogical relation is a specific relation that does not fall under a logical, linguistic, or psychological system. Dialogical relations constitute a special type of semantic relations, whose members can only be complete utterances (either regarded as complete or potentially complete), behind which stand (and in which are expressed) real or potentially real speech subjects, authors of the given utterances.[24]

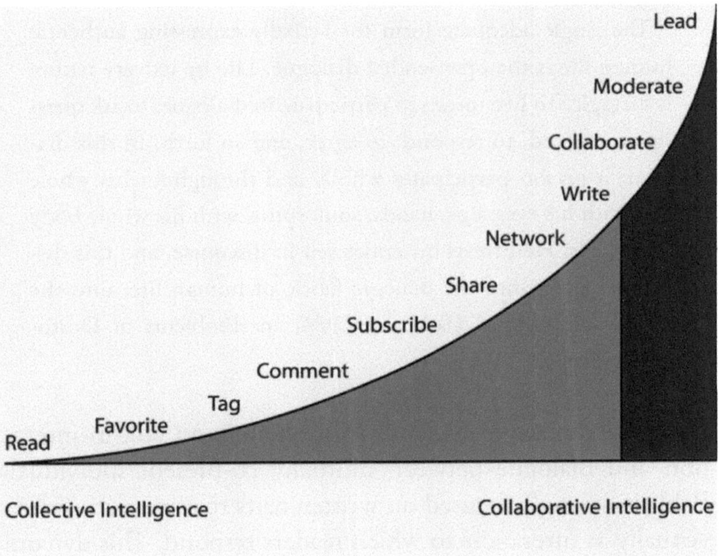

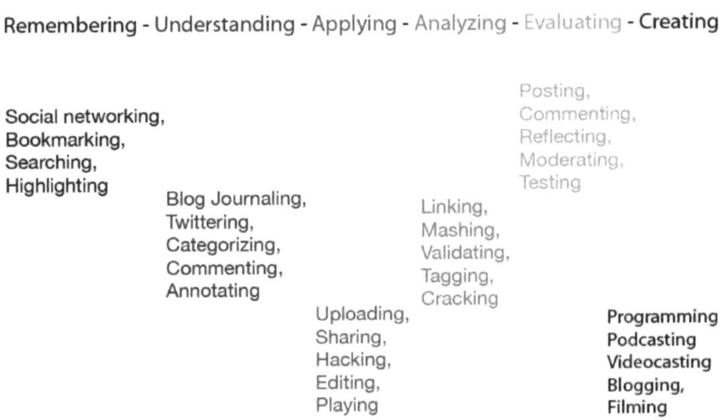

9 Power law of participation

10 Bloom's Revised "Digital" Taxonomy by A. Churches, 2001

> "The single adequate form for verbally expressing authentic human life is the open-ended dialogue. Life by its very nature is dialogic. To live means to participate in dialogue: to ask questions, to heed, to respond, to agree, and so forth. In this dialogue a person participates wholly and throughout his whole life: with his eyes, lips, hands, soul, spirit, with his whole body and deeds. He invests his entire self in discourse, and this discourse enters into the dialogic fabric of human life, into the world symposium" (Bakhtin, 1984, In: Problems of Dostoevsky's Poetics, 293).

As we can see dialogism focuses mainly on talk-in-interaction and dialogue between mutually co-present individuals. Bakhtin strongly focused on written texts that were considered virtually as utterances to which readers respond. This dynamic conception of texts has gained fresh momentum with the advent of the Internet and its opportunities for infinite hypertexts, stressing new forms of intertextuality, which, in simple terms, is the shaping of texts' meanings by other texts. How relevant dialogism is in current Web 2.0 developments can be observed in the blogosphere and wikisphere, where the text's physical structures are constantly in a productive dialogue with its user/makers and its congruent texts.

However, language in use is invariably indexical, allusive and incomplete. Hence utterance must rely on contextualization of 'non-verbal' signs such as voice characteristics, gestures, facial expressions, body movements and postures. Shortcomings of purely verbal communication ("language bias") become even more evident in the meaning and sense making processes in online communication.

However, to fully understand the complexity of computer-mediated communication, we need to consider the interdependent epistemological, ontological and functional aspects in it. That is, language used as a medium for example in phone calls over the Internet cannot be separated from the a) communicator; b) technology; c) function and usage. Possible disturbances that might occur at one or at all three levels are merely considered a technological shortcoming. Yet we know that synchronous communication processes require a vast repertoire of skills in intrapersonal and interpersonal processing, listening, observing, speaking, questioning, analyzing, and evaluating. Communication is social interaction, and thus it cannot be broken down into a simple information transforming process, for example the basic sender-signal-channel-receiver model,

> in which ideas are taken as objects and thought as the manipulation of objects. An important part of this metaphor is that memory is 'storage.' Communication in that metaphor is the following: ideas are objects that you can put into words (or store as bits), so that language is seen as a container for ideas, and you send ideas in words over a circuit, a channel of communication to someone else who then extracts the ideas from the words (Lakoff, 1995, 116).

Information and control are closely related concepts within systems theory (like cybernetics). Ideas can be extracted and can exist independently of people, in a computer, for example. As a result, information and its processing can exist in a disembodied form. Accordingly, the meaning (content) of information is set apart as irrelevant to the determination of its value in terms of quantitative measures. But, cybernetics is also about "purposiveness, goals, information flows, decision-making control processes and feedback (properly defined) at all levels of living systems."[25]

This brings us back to the fundamental discernment that information from the standpoint of information sciences is defined by its existence as a bit—in Bateson's formulation, "a difference that makes a difference". We can go even further, arguing that information is the "energy" in the system that functions within the control processes of a network economy. In corporate culture information and communication is conceived as an element of control within a complex system of hierarchical order and manipulative control mechanisms. Control of information and communication equates with control of code, leading again to fundamental questions: "Who is the owner of the code, where is it stored, and what are the consequences of misuse?"

Crowdsourcing is a good example of how malleable the principles of open source and exchange culture become ("you contribute something in order to get something better in return"), not least triggered by leveraging the mass communication and collaboration enabled by Web 2.0 technologies to make profit at the expense of each individual contributor. Thus principles of open dialogue and shared networking cannot be separated from the ideologically driven market mechanism. What has originally been conceived as economy of scale where there is no exchange of commodities but immaterial value has only recently been distorted by the announcement that the Bertelsmann publishing house, part of the multinational Random House group, is to print a German version of Wikipedia. This commercially-driven act torpedoes the main principles of a participatory online encyclopedia in multiple ways: a) a voluntarily co-authored, open and dynamic web-based knowledge repository cannot be transferred into static print media; b) open content is free for everyone, whereas the printed version is not; c) a book version is limited in size, scalability, actuality, distribution and (closed) format; d) the argument that a printed version would reach the poor and non-connected does not hold true in the specific case of a German version (and I rather doubt this would be true for other countries with a high number of illiterate people); e) even though the GNU Free Documentation License allows commercial reuse, there is a profound difference between generating new business models on the basis of keeping the source code open and selling a book product that is genuinely non-modifiable. From this example we can learn how exploitable "gift culture" is and how subtly market mechanisms are cloaked in the name and symbols of common wealth.

In other words, it is not the content being concentrated but the economic value of content. MySpace, Facebook, and many other businesses have realized that they can provide free production and dissemination tools but maintain ownership over the resulting products. The long tail (Anderson 2004) of the niche strategy of certain businesses (e.g. Amazon) allow them to realize significant profit out of selling small volumes of hard-to-find items to many customers, instead of only selling large volumes of a reduced number of popular items. It appears that the fundamental economic characteristics of Web 2.0 is the distribution of production into the hands of the many and the concentration of the economic rewards into the hands of the few:

> By posting User Content to any part of the Site, you automatically grant, and you represent and warrant that you have the right to grant, to the Company an irrevocable, perpetual,

> non-exclusive, transferable, fully paid, worldwide license (with the right to sublicense) to use, copy, publicly perform, publicly display, reformat, translate, excerpt (in whole or in part) and distribute such User Content... (see http://www.facebook.com/terms.php).

Nicholas Carr calls this a sharecropper system, in which the crowd operates happily in an attention economy while their overseers operate happily in a cash economy. In this view, the attention economy does not operate separately from the cash economy; it is simply a means of creating cheap inputs for the cash economy.

Coevally similar power laws can be applied to social software group activities (Fig. 9). Here the vast majority of users do not actively engage with a given group; most tend to be free riders upon community value. Taking a closer look at the different web practices of diverse user groups, we see that a low threshold of participation amounts to collective intelligence, whereas on the other hand high engagement complies with a different form of collaborative intelligence.

The concept of collective intelligence can be described as an emergent property of collective social systems whereas collaborative intelligence is the ability to produce synergy in one's relationship with that environment. In a group-oriented process of working together towards greater shared understanding, for example in Open Space Technology, dialogic forms use and evoke collaborative intelligence most vividly.

However, as we all know, it is not easy to do something creative with diverse opinions and experiences, and by experience, the disposition to settle for lowest-common-denominator agreements does all too often prevail in group-oriented processes. In communities of practice (Wenger 1998), the individual engages as an active participant in the practices of social communities and in the construction of his/her identity through these communities. A major activity of a democratic community is then developing the skills, procedures, and attitudes needed for people to jointly create through their diversity. These democratic tools, the diversity and independence of opinions, the decentralization and aggregation of knowledge, still hold a notion of hope that the community's thinking becomes more wise, their collective behavior more intelligent and successful (Fig. 10).

5 Transitory Processes

There has been an ongoing discussion for several years now on the relationship of art and science in educational and professional contexts. Is this just another attempt to put an old fashion into new clothes? I do not think so, because this time the arguments do not constitute an attempt to make a qualitative distinction between universities or higher institutions of art, design and media. Nor is there a fundamental dispute involved whether the artistic singularity of an artefact or scientific objectivity claims to have more epistemic value.

In search of significant sources nourishing the current discourse, paradigmatic changes in the process of renewing and preserving the conditions of cultural self-organization are key to a major shift in how we construct knowledge, technology and cultural memory. It concerns institutional forms as well as the individual.

One of the standpoints is to consider a revival of the "Leonardo principle". A second standpoint might close the chapter on the relationship between art and science for the benefit of scientific-economic prosperity, whereas a third engages with the question of how cultural, intellectual and spiritual fields are prerequisite to evolutions in art, science and technology. My affinity is with the third, although some of the related issues also apply to the other positions.

Many questions derive from the context of audiovisual restructuring of knowledge and communication areas in interrelated and cooperative fields molding into novel forms of interdisciplinary design, such as BANG design, whose acronym stands for the basic modules of our world (B=Bits, A=Atoms,

N=Neurons, G=Genes).[1] This field will be extended by neurophysiological research into cognition and perception, not to be confused with the ontological and philosophical terminology of cognition and perception. In conjunction with media- and biotechnological industrialization of codes, concepts and design in the educational context of art and science have been renewed.

Can both art and science learn from each other, and, if so, at what and for what? Do both act in the same framework of design and conceptualization, as some of the new generation of media artists suggest in their explorative approach? Would it make sense to exchange curricular modules between specific study programs?

Narrowing down the thematic frame, one crucial question remains: Which of the teaching and learning fields between art (in terms of audiovisual media design and media use) and science (in terms of research of audiovisual cognition, development of formalized models containing complex mediality and prototyping of media structures) can be formulated?

The paradigmatic closeness of art, science, the economy and politics might suggest a consistent media evolution based on media convergence, yet this does not give us a satisfying answer. The point is if, and if so, to what extent does it become meaningful to reformulate the very densely organized media evolutionary areas to make plausible and distinct the differences between artistic and scientific education?

In that respect it will not make sense to reactivate old habits of distinguishing between art and sciences. Current developments in media and biotechnology, neuroscience and cognition research, but also in humanity and cultural science, demonstrate the interrelatedness of knowledge creation and knowledge representation. These developments cope with the complexity of design and research thus being of a transferable structure. This principle similarly applies to art and science. In fact, novel theoretical delineations of model, game and communication knowledge in different contexts has changed the theoretical architecture if we consider the impact of second-order cybernetic and radical constructivism (von Foerster), positions in Endophysics (Rössler),[2] concepts of neuronal networks, and fuzzy logic and boundary management concepts mediating between disciplines and product developments.

However, these radical changes in cognition and design architecture have had less impact on learning and knowledge organization thus far. A conceptual lag can be identified in both teaching and research. We know, for example, that not only knowledge and media technology is changing rapidly, but learning attitudes and styles are also changing fluidly across different technologies, interfaces and modes of interaction. As a consequence institutions react with a stronger emphasis on project and praxis orientation. It is not so much about how specific themes relate to a subject or university-specific didactics. The crucial issue concerns the way and to what extent the changing organization of perception and cognition, designing, processing and selection is teachable, and if it is teachable, how it can be conducted.

If we accept one of the prevailing concepts in 20th century theory, art would predominantly be created by its viewer and users; based on the economy of attentiveness and the market, a serious discussion on curricular changes would be useless. In other words art cannot be taught if it is to "potential" art producers. Would education then solely be a privilege for curators, patrons, visitors of museums and galleries, cultural managers who create, reflect and provide affirmative market behavior? Obviously there is still a dichotomy between institutional education and self-education. In fact, the educational landscape and discourse relating to art has long since evolved to cover a much wider range of important issues to be explored such as media and popular culture. "Takeover – who is doing the art of tomorrow", the topics of Ars Electronica 2001,[3] strove for a broader discussion on new manifestations of art and fluid learning arrangements driven by the dynamics of digital revolution. The dynamism of "Takeover" does not originate from traditional art practice and mediation but rather from largely heterogeneous, rhizome-like structures and networks of remotely connected individuals and online communities. The common goal of these activities pertaining to evolving culture is not merely a distant-reflective kind of reaction to techno-social changes; in fact, these activities constitute and develop further this genuine field.

Digital network culture has not only been changing the modes of media production and distribution: it coevally conveys emerging models of cooperation, communication and interaction by accumulating various ideas, talents and capabilities. Hence, the tasks of tomorrow's artist is that of an intermediary, a catalyst between diverse fields of knowledge, ways of thinking, social models and solution strategies. The protagonists of this development, hackers, software artists, media and knowledge designers who are irrespectively showing strong commitment in the face of considerable risk, are opening up new territories in which their role and their scope of action have not yet been fully explored. This alludes to critical inquiry, research and development in socio-political and scientific (biotechnology and genetic engineering) contexts.

Interestingly yet not surprisingly, the conventional artistic discourse has been cultivating and maintaining a self-referential and affirmative practice among galleries, magazines, investors, dealers and critics. The corporate image of the artwork has long since replaced the artwork itself. A good example is the "Institutional Critique", an art practice in which often only advanced artists, theorists, historians, and critics can participate. Due to its highly sophisticated understanding of modern art and society, as part of a privileged discourse like that of any other specialized form of knowledge, it has predominantly yielded alienated and marginalized viewers. Net art in contrast has explored the field in a much broader context by exemplifying the work of art as a process, as opposed to a conception of art as object making. Since net art is "immaterial", commodity value is replaced by utility value: i.e., the principles of the net economy are based on an economy of scale where there is no scarcity of goods. Thus the added value is not generated by a thousand copies of the same "product" but instead by the "exchange value" based on each different source of information and not on each individual copy (cf. Ghosh 1998).[4]

In his lecture "Science as an Open Source Process", Friedrich Kittler[5] argues that the liberty of science rises and falls in parallel with source code liberation. Only then will science become a university. In that sense, the definition of university implies, differently from in closed or secret research centers, that the knowledge must circulate and be accessible without the protection of patents and copyright issues. Media convergence gives us the opportunity to dissolve the media-technical boundaries between natural scientific, technical and cultural knowledge.

In my reflection on transitory processes in art, science and education, I will refer to Roger Fidler's Mediamorphosis, which describes the material, logical and cultural practical use and developments of media. Art and science are dependent on these morphic surroundings by inventing, developing and generating new ones. Relating to this dimension of mediamorphic events, I would like to add the following quotation:

> Cyberspace... enables its audience not merely to observe a reality, but to enter it and experience it as if it were real.... Whereas film is used to show a reality to an audience, cyberspace is used to give a virtual body, and a role, to everyone in the audience. Print and radio tell; stage and film show; cyberspace embodies.[6]

Questions arising in this specific context relate to teachable contiguity in media production and design, the ratio between subject and media-specific teaching, and how both can be applied in a dynamic, reciprocal mode.

Media evolution has been taking place over many centuries as specialization and fragmentation of sensual perception, communication and concepts of truth. It has been a long history of segregation of multisensoric options in human self-organization. The effects of this process of specialization and disjuncture have generated particularly strong systems such as paintings, scripture, sciences, aesthetics and so on. This has led to a material and mental disparity to which can be assigned the same texture and facture and distinctive canonic differences as with institutions, iconoclastic and iconophilic cultures. Some of the distinctive systems that arose out of this process, such as the privileged status of reading over vision, have come under pressure by multimodal and multicodal forms of production, perception and reception. Alongside the media's evolutionary "agenda", post-modernist and post-structuralist concepts (Derrida, Foucault, Lévinas) and tendencies of individualization in socio-cultural changes and use of the new media are frequently being conceptualized as a dichotomy of unleashing ("deboundarization"). However, in the current media discourse there are tendencies to discover media practice from another perspective, which means that a connection between persistence and recombination of social structuring and social practices can be seen as a model for social change. This model is predicated on the hypothesis that the use of new media is based on given social structures and social practices. With respect to tendencies like individualization and globalization, the social potential of new media such as weblogs[7] offers distinct forms of media use within different social practices, including the strengthening of the latter as well as doing without them.

With regard to media-related functions and their proliferation, the extension of computer technology is irreversibly encoded in delocalized media and electronic networks as part of culture and society as distributed and diversified systems. A constituent factor in this process is media convergence or integration. Alongside the media synthetic approach to merging different media into one, we can identify another important attempt towards multisensory perception. The visual sense, the faculty of vision, gets back its vast cultural spectrum ("from *Lascaux* to the *Virtual Museum*") and in parallel the interface changes into a multisensory one. This epoch-making electronic and fiber-optic based media convergence has ceased the history of media divergence. From now on, the point is how different media functions, whether in a pure or crossover mode, come into play.

Screenager, a term first coined by Douglas Rushkoff in his 1997 book *Playing the Future,* is a technologically savvy young person living next door with audiovisual gadgets and interfaces, where he/she interacts in a mediated setting of learning, entertainment, peer bonding and play. Is the interconnected "mediaspace a co-operative dream, made up of the combined projections of everyone who takes part",[8] or do these trade-offs speak to a wider set of socio-cultural implications and consequences in light of an education "close to reality"?

Taking into account the next generation of students there is now a way to cope with hybrid digital learning cultures. What was with all those demands for change in higher education institutional settings? Although several educational outreach activities have been undertaken since then, the mediation paradigm ("blended/hybrid modes of teaching and learning") often fails on the basics.

If we interpret art and science as two dimensions relating to (post)modernist and interface culture, the prerequisites in defining a new curriculum change significantly. It would thus demand another structure of design capabilities corresponding with an all-encompassing model of knowledge design. Thus, many of the practices and alternative viewpoints these theories claim, in terms of adaptive, flexible and transgressive forms of learning and developing new contextual abilities, would likewise change artistic and scientific educational processes. The most fundamental macro-question in communication, media theory, and cultural theory is the nature of mediation, which means that we have always been in language, in symbolic systems, and we know our lived-in world through language, discourse, and signs, not by immediate access to "things in themeselves" (Kant). The primacy of mediation in any theoretical model is milieu, medium, structure and system of mediation. Hence artistic practice changes significantly into mediation between the viewer and the subject, between "art" and "life", media, technique and expression, art and institutions, copyright and artwork.

Over the last two decades, we have learned about dissipative structures in biology, fractal and chaos theory, network and self-organization theory, yet with little impact on academic institutional teaching and learning culture. With the notion of social technologies, the current accompanying transformation process from single authorship to co-authorship, public versus person-to-person communication, contributions versus display, has become virulent in the net activism of the 1990's that links in many ways with the social or socially critical processes of the 1960's and 70's (e.g. U. Eco's "open" works of art and J. Beuys's concept of "social sculpture" relating plastic creativity to socio-political activities, K. Galloway and S. Rabinowitz's "Hole-In-Space" regarding telematics and telepresence). Current social software developments are merging the socio-political and media-technological towards a democratizing and participatory media approach.

By applying this to learning processes in a digital age, one of the main questions is how the increased recognition of interconnections in differing fields of knowledge, systems and ecology theories is perceived in light of learning tasks. Alternative theories deriving from chaos, self-organization and social network theories suggest that we can no longer personally experience and acquire the learning that we need to act. We derive our competence from forming connections. Chaos, as a science, recognizes the connection of everything to everything.[9] The butterfly analogy highlights the challenge of how we deal with sensitive dependence on initial conditions that profoundly impact what we learn and how we act based on our learning. As for social-network theories, Albert-László Barabási states that "nodes always compete for connections because links represent survival in an interconnected world".[10] This competition is largely dulled within a personal learning network, but the placing of value on certain nodes over others is a reality. Connections between disparate ideas and fields can create new innovations. This amplification of learning, knowledge and understanding through the extension of a personal network is the epitome of a new learning culture.

Multiple Perspectives

The creation of multiperspective perception does not necessarily require interdisciplinarity, which sometimes disguises academic disciplinary thinking. Moreover it should be a process of reorientation and aggregation of subject-specific knowledge and coherences, yet under the premises of audiovisual introspection of our cultures through mediality. The reference system to which the process of knowledge creation adheres could be easily extended if we consider e.g. the traditional panel not only as a technique of representation but also from the viewpoint of techniques of (self) observance, which means the cooperative integration of acoustics and optics, mathematics and epistemology, neurophysiology and communication theory, media evolution and visual sciences.

I think it is important to define (audio-) visual education no longer through either exposed or archived representativeness. Neither are there economic arguments to make plausible a separation of text and image, generated and displayed in the same medium, nor other acceptable objections, whether they stem from platonic reasoning or similar epistemological coinage, to deny images the same intelligible and explanatory potential that has been ascribed to scripture and text over the centuries.

Computer-generated visibility applies to encoded data representations that simultaneously show a typographic simulation and a visualization. The collapse of the classical semiotic reference system of "signification" (Peirce) has been superseded by the sober conclusion that "[i]mages do no more represent world but data", or, as Peter Galison puts it, "Images scatter into data, data scatter into images."[11]

GoogleEarth is a good example of how the cartography of the world increasingly flows into the cartography of the internet. "World" becomes downloadable, navigable and manipulable. Programming (technique), interface (aesthetic) and interactivity (human-machine, human-human interaction/social dimension) merge into new modes of production, perception and reception. Since human cognition strongly relies on visual patterns, the enormous amount of data demands new visualization strategies. Simulation is an attempt to model a real-life situation on a computer so that it can be studied to see how the system works.

Another important aspect relates to communicative skills and competences as dialogical principles. Changing perspectives also means communicative interdependency between the respective knowledge and skills in relation to social praxis. If we acknowledge the fact that knowledge, competences and skills are circularly determined, long-term planned curricula would no longer work for teaching in art or science.

Courses of instruction claim to be flexible and adaptive, and as a consequence, new dependencies emerge between institutions, processes of accreditation and the actual course developments.

Another assumption pertains to the rhetorically well-trained relationship between ethics and aesthetics, or following Aristotle's formulation, phronesis (mitigation) and aesthesis (sense perception). Perhaps one should avoid making the mistake of constantly serving to fulfill both, e.g. media-technological and artistic skills, mediality and aesthetics. It would be a fatal backslide into premodern concepts of harmonic principles, which are from my point of view, from a media-theoretical standpoint, no longer applicable in contemporary contexts.

Complexity

An all-encompassing final thought to consider is that of complexity, meaning an uncountable dimension of unpredictable events.[12] With regard to thinking critically and productively about media form, content, and context, it is difficult to say whether it will be ever possible to educate media competence that fulfils the demands of complexity. It seems to me that it is more appropriate to develop sensitivity in managing complex situations and demands. That is to say that neither artists nor scientists are able to predict if and how their ideas and concepts will be accepted, copied, evaluated and varied upon. Artists by their nature seem to be more dependent on the selecting milieu of appreciation than might be said of scientists. In my opinion, thinking and doing are rather isolated qualities in artistic areas that need to be strategically developed for the competitive art and gallery business. This empowers artists on the one hand to display a sensibility for complex demands "just in time"; on the other hand many promising artistic careers have failed to cope with these specific demands. Indeed, scientists have developed a certain kind of sensibility for complexity as well, but how they differ from artistic milieus is a peculiar attitude of prudence towards provenance, causation and precondition that strongly relates to thinking in systematic order and theoretical boundaries.

Both of these, current practices of sensibility for complexity in media arts and the sensibility for stringent reasoning in media, cognitive and communication sciences, could, if flexibly applied in learning processes, stimulate the co-designing of novel hybrid forms in theory and practice.

Practices

How can these expectations meet the challenges in learning and teaching contexts? The following are proposals based on applied research.

– *Modularization*

This is to increase the system's responsiveness to changing skill needs. Modules in audiovisual, media-technological, cognitive and communicative areas are easier to revise and update than full courses. The pedagogical changes implied are to encourage more student-centered, self-regulated, participative and active learning.

Modules can be defined based on projects or tasks to encourage learning and to develop "transferable skills" such as personal autonomy, responsibility, decision-making and the ability to exercise initiative. A modular structure is used to support independent study and individual student needs. This should be thought of and realized as a revocable, temporally limited structure within adaptive learning processes.

– *Projects*

Project work emphasizes explorative learning and research-based design in knowledge-building communities and organizations[13] supported by socio-cognitive as well as technological dynamics. As for socio-cognitive dynamics, community knowledge and collective responsibility equally foster individual achievements and contributions to shared, top-level goals of the organization.

Democratizing knowledge means that diversity and divisional differences represented in any organization do not lead to separations along knowledge have/have-not or innovator/non-innovator lines. In order to achieve symmetry in knowledge advancement, expertise is distributed within and between communities. To give knowledge is to get knowledge. Early acquaintance with such technological, theoretical and communicative complexity advances thinking and acting in cooperative design processes.

– *Field Practice*

The dynamics of knowledge creation and distribution alongside the side-effects of neoliberal labor policy requires critical and creative thinking more than ever before. Internships in diverse scientific, economic, artistic, public and administrative working fields offer the possibility of learning and knowledge transfer in some of the professional areas with which teachers and learners are less familiar. In fact, new technologies require a much broader spectrum of competences, skills and knowledge such as social communicative competences, contextual abilities, flexibility and attendance to work and practice in collaborative environments, a disposition to challenge the ongoing paradigm shift in the knowledge society, an openness to socio-cultural diversity, a wide range of ICT skills through work or study, and practical and theoretical skills in media and visual literacy. The need for such experts is not confined to any of the cultural segments.

– *Tools*

How strongly do social software tools impact on current practices in e-learning in general, and second, what are the implications for the student's mode of interaction (social factor), aesthetics (interface culture) and techniques (interoperability)? Some of my findings derive from actual research on learning ecology and multiple reality constructions, which reciprocally both affect and are affected by multiple facets in socio-economic and culturally encoded concepts of living. One of these aspects relates to competitiveness in a global job market, which is in fact the driving force behind the concept of lifelong learning and the prevailing motivation of our students to continuously qualify. Interestingly, yet not surprisingly, connectivity has expanded into fluid forms of networking on the basis of immaterial value exchange. Shared spaces where people can communicate, exchange and aggregate information, co-author and co-create areas of common interest, need flexible and adjustable arrangements in our study approach over distance. Some of the key problems we have identified include the limitations of interactions with structured tools; another confinement relates to interface design, communication and learning tools.

Learning Management Systems are suitable when content and information provision is key to the learning strategy: however when interactions and connections are in the foreground then social tools are required. As an alternative to *conventional* tools we are now testing how modular tools can expand functionality; to what extent social tools encourage individual expression and connect learners and content; how synchronous tools can be integrated; and how learner-centered tools encourage learning ecology. The types of tools suggested include Blogs, Wikis, Virtual Worlds, social tools, networking tools, collaborative spaces, and connection-making protocols (RSS and Atom). But how do these alternatives provide the learner with control of the type of content explored, and how do they explore to effectively meet their learning goals?

– *Student requirements*

The core infrastructure of the international study program contains a group Blog where students feed-in study and research topic relevant information. In addition, group work over a distance in an international setting relating to project work topics is either organized in Blogs or in password-protected communities, which allow flexible information aggregation and dynamic knowledge construction. Spontaneous and organized one-to-one, one-to-many or many-to-many conversations are conducted over the Internet (e.g. via Skype). Photo and video sharing tools, podcasts and virtual world habitats are like-minded modes of expression. Especially in international and multilingual user groups it is interesting to see how local interests and cultural idiosyncrasies can be refashioned[14] and re-contextualized in the predominantly English speaking communities (Fig. 1).

A tendency towards social networking tools (StudiVZ and Facebook) can be observed as community specific phenomena. It seems that the study and online communities originally conceived as an integral part of either proprietary or open source based Learning Management Systems can no longer support adequate preconditions that would serve the users' need to either randomly or purposefully connect, share and communicate for different occasions at the same time, and they are thus becoming obsolete. This means the community with which I am connected and potentially could be connected in future by means of social networking tools continuously expands and converges into software clusters stimulating multitasking and proposing living in (on) the net. Smart mobile technologies that would create another dimension of spatiotemporal relationships between connected users have not yet achieved similar Asian (especially Japanese[15]) standards.

Immediacy and spontaneous action and reaction, open discourse and dialogue, are prerequisites in creative learning processes. What might be inspiring in a group discussion during a seminar or workshop does not necessarily lead to similar experiences in communication processes through virtual technologies. The lack of physical co-presence in online interaction, and the demands placed on us by others to be responsive and participatory, can be summed up as issues of self-presentation and the negotiation of presence availability. One of the unique challenges of self-presentation in mediated environments deals with the presentation of intention and sincerity, or authenticity. Meta-level communication plays an important part in helping us to convey our authenticity, but it also permits us irony, parody and other self-referential communication. Considering the nonlinguistic aspects such facial and physical gestures it becomes apparent that we do not always say what we mean: Friendster[16] (a social networking service) involves "fakesters" or "pretendsters", meaning that many members introduce fake profiles.

Some of the viable solutions developed thus far have been to encourage members to get to know each other in semi-public contexts such as discussions and listings, where community expectations can serve as a check on credibility (e.g. Wikis).

– *Dialogue:*

The most prevalent communication tools split into synchronous Internet telephony (VoIP) and asynchronous e-mail communication. As the combination of both means of communication allows for sincerity, privacy and efficiency according to the topics of discussion, other means such as public posts on Blogs or Message Boards are pre-selected information meant to engage a wider audience through open dialogue.

Mentors and experts joining in during project work, international seminars, online discussions and courses are usually acquainted with specific communication tools, means and methods. Learning processes that have been originally organized and structured at moderated expert forums based on a knowledge-building process between students, docents, experts, and tutors have gradually shifted into the blogosphere and social bookmarking (del.icio.us) for the purpose of extending one's own network and sharing knowledge. In addition, podcasts and videocasts are becoming increasingly important documentations for student-centered learning, nevertheless involving a rather time-consuming editing approach.

– *Content:*

Content sharing and co-creation coevally takes place in open, accessible and restricted online environments. However, course content, which is prone to copyright and other licenses such as Creative Commons, will be mainly delivered in restricted areas. In that respect we can make a distinction between dynamic and cooperatively generated forms of knowledge aggregation through publicly accessible Wikis or Blogs, and restricted areas of online course modules, which are shared and organized entirely between enrolled students and docents. The key question is how both forms, dynamic "on-the-fly" creation of contents and elaborated course modules containing clear assessment, assignment and evaluation criteria, impact reciprocally and beneficially on content creation as such.

The specific constellation of the international MA program in the form of a jointly developed curriculum originally intended course delivery and access via local and university-specific open source based LMS or proprietary solutions. This changed during the project lifetime and activities as the course contents and resources became increasingly dispersed parallel to project working groups' specific media usage. The mixed media structure of connected but independent tools, means and methods resembles the study organization, structure and objectives inasmuch as the pedagogical principles pursue Deleuze's thinking[17]— a society based on rhizome-like networks.

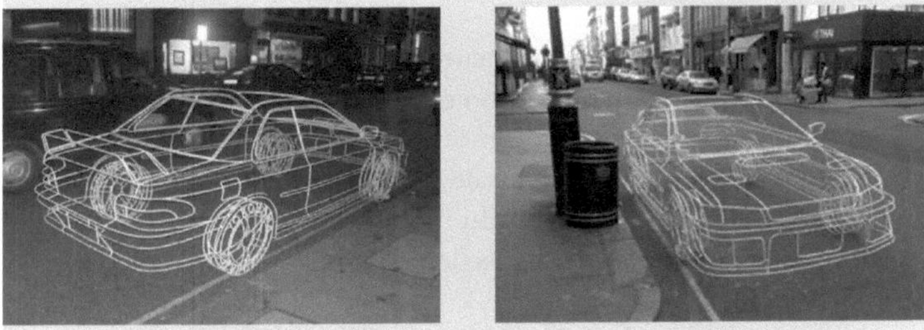

1 Remediation: Wire frame sculpture by Benedict Radcliffe;
Avatar 3D print from Second Life; Real - Second Life persiflage

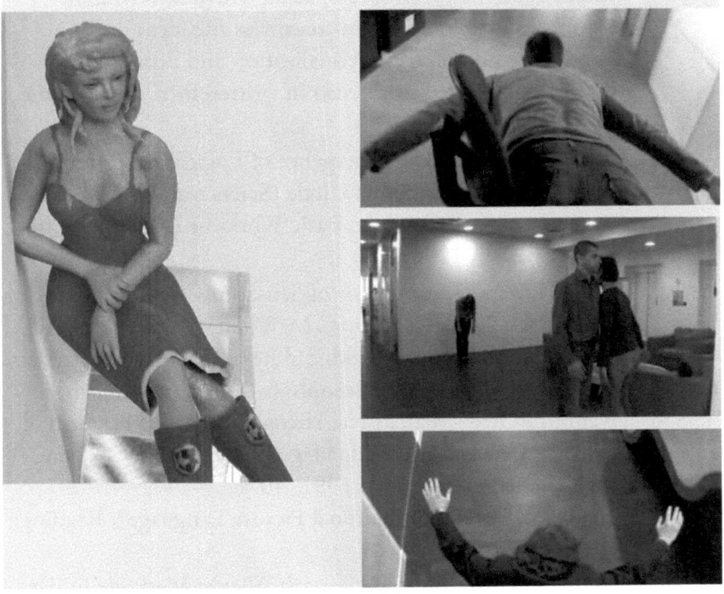

Notes

1

1 cf. http://www.mundaneum.be (6.5.2008).
2 Otlet, Paul. "L'Education et les Instituts du Palais Mondial" (Mundaneum), Publication No 121. Bruxelles: UIA, 1926.
3 Otlet, Paul. Monde: essaie d'universalisme – connaissance du monde; sentiment du monde; action organisée et plan du monde; Bruxelles: Editions du Mundaneum, 1935.
4 Heuvel van den, Charles. "Visualizing the Organization and Dissemination of Knowledge: Paul Otlet's Sketches in the Mundaneum", 2005. http://informationvisualization.typepad.com/sigvis/2005/07/visualizations_.html
5 Late in his life, Otlet began to develop what he called an Atlas Mundaneum (Encyclopaedia Universalis Mundaneum), in which he sought to express the ideas on knowledge organization, visualization and dissemination that he had treated in extenso in written form in his Traité de documentation (1934).
6 Nozick, Robert. "The Emergence of Logical Empiricism: From 1900 to the Vienna Circle (Science and Philosophy in the Twentieth Century: Basic Works of Logical Empiricism)"; 321 ff, 1996.
7 Mach, Ernst. "The Analysis of Sensations" 1897. Dover Edition, 1959; Translation: by C M Williams and Sydney Waterlow. First Chapter reproduced here: http://www.marxists.org/reference/subject/philosophy/works/ge/mach.htm
8 Neurath, Otto. "Statistische Hieoglyphen", In: Haller und Kinross, Gesammelte Bildpädagogische Schriften, Wien: Hölder-Pichler-Tempsky, 1991, 40.
9 Neurath, Otto. "International Picture Language", Reading: 1980, 18.
10 Neurath, Otto, Bildstatistik nach Wiener Methode in der

Schule, Wien: 1933.

11 Neurath, Otto, On Visual Education, Survey Graphic, vol. 26, no. 1 (January, 1937), 25.

2

1 http://www.bfi.org/node/25 (10.5.2008).

2 Fuller, Richard Buckminister, SYNERGETICS I

3 http://earth.google.com/outreach/index.html (5.5.2008).

4 From Rwanda to Darfur: Lessons Learned? By Gerald Caplan; www.globalpolicy.org/security/issues/sudan/2006/0112lessons.htm (5.5.2008).

5 http://www.holocaust-trc.org/edu_holocaust.htm (5.5.2008).

6 cf. http://www.softcinema.net/form.htm (10.5.2008).

7 Benjamin, Walter, "Unpacking My Library." In Illuminations, pp. 59-67.

8 Definitions and Rationale for Visualizations, http://www.siggraph.org/education/materials/HyperVis (10.5.2008).

9 Volcanoes may reveal secrets through 'song', http://environment.newscientist.com/article/dn9711.html (10.5.2008)

10 http://www.aec.at/en/archives/prix_archive/prix_winner.asp?iProjectID=1 (10.5.2008).

11 ACM SIGGRAPH Computer Graphics archive Volume 22 , Issue 4 (August 1988), pp. 327 – 334.

12 http://www.visual-literacy.org/periodic_table/periodic_table.html, (10.5.2008).

13 http://www.youtube.com/watch?v=qYGC-zh2XH8 (10.5.2008).

14 www.uni-weimar.de/medien/ar/Pub/Slides/ISMAR05/ISMAR05.pdf, or http://www.youtube.com/watch?v=0nDf5AOJWy4 (10.5.2008).

15 Laszlo Moholy-Nagy, The New Vision and Abstract of an Artist, New York: Wittenborn, 1947, p. 79.

16 cf. Hodges, Alan, Turing Internet Scrap Book, http://www.turing.org.uk, (10.5.2008).
17 Florian Cramer, Concepts, Notations, Software, Art, 2002, http://www.netzliteratur.net/cramer/concepts_notations_software_art.html
18 cf. Heckl, Wolfgang, Das Unsichtbare sichtbar machen, In: Iconic Turn, Köln: Dumont, 2004, pp. 128-142.
19 http://netzspannung.org/database/104954/de (10.5.2008).

3

1 Martin Dodge and Rob Kitchin, The Ethics of Forgetting in an Age of Pervasive Computing 1, http://www.casa.ucl.ac.uk/working_papers/paper92.pdf (16.12.2007).
2 Metaverse Roadmap: Pathways to the 3D Web, http://metaverseroadmap.org/ (12.12.2007).
3 How Many Bytes in Human Memory? by Ralph C. Merkle. This article first appeared in Foresight Update No. 4, October 1988.
4 cf. *As We May Think,* http://www.theatlantic.com/doc/194507/bush/ (20.11.2007).
5 cf. The Warhol Collections Archive, http://www.warhol.org/collections/archives.html (18.12.2007).
6 *MyLifeBits: Fulfilling the Memex Vision,* Gemmell, Jim, Bell, Gordon, Lueder, Roger, Drucker, Steven, and Wong, Curtis, ACM Multimedia '02, December 1-6, 2002, Juan-les-Pins, France, pp. 235-238.
7 cf. http://www.0100101110101101.org/home/performances/ (20.12.2007).
8 BBC news, 2002, http://news.bbc.co.uk/1/hi/sci/tech/1789157.stm
9 cf. Iconic Turn, http://www.iconic-turn.de/ (16.12.2007).
10 Sousveillance (inverse surveillance) as a way to balance

the increasing (and increasingly one-sided) surveillance. http://wearcam.org/sousveillance.htm (08.09.2007)

11 Tutorial slides on assumptions, the formalism and the mathematics behind non-zero-sum game theory. http://www.autonlab.org/tutorials/nonzerosum06.pdf (10.09.2007)

12 Pareto distribution, named after the Italian economist Vilfredo Pareto (1848 - 1926), is a power law probability distribution that coincides with social, scientific, geophysical and many other types of observable phenomena.

4

1 http://www.se.rit.edu/~jrv/research/ar/introduction.html (10.5.2008).

2 Stelarc, Prosthetics, Robotics and Remote Existence: Post-revolutionary Strategies. Leonardo, Vol. 24, No. 5 (1991), pp. 591-595.

3 ScienceDaily, That's Not My Hand! How The Brain Can Be Fooled Into Feeling A Fake Limb, http://www.sciencedaily.com/releases/2004/07 (10.5.2008).

4 Lenggenhager et al., Video Ergo Sum: Manipulating Bodily Self-Consciousness, Science 24 August 2007: 1096-1099.

5 Jean Baudrillard, The Conspiracy of Art: Manifestos, Interviews. Edited by Sylvere Lotringer and Translated by Ames Hodges. New York: Semiotext(e), 2005.

6 Bagdikian, Ben, The New Media Monopoly, Boston: Beacon Press, 2004.

7 http://www.saffo.com/essays/essay_farewellinfo.pdf (10.5.2008).

8 http://www.ubiq.com/hypertext/weiser/ACMInteractions2.html (10.5.2008).

9 http://www.research.philips.com/technologies/misc/

homelab/downloads/homelab_365.pdf (10.5.2008).
10 cf. Garfinkel, Harold, Ethnomethodology's Program, New York: Rowman and Littlefield, 2002.
11 http://snibbe.com/scott/ (10.5.2008).
12 Voronoi diagrams, cf. http://www.voronoi.com (10.5.2008).
13 cf. http://www.cs.unm.edu/~sheppard/proxemics.htm (10.5.2008).
14 cf. Nick Yee's research on social phenomena in MMORPGs, http://www.nickyee.com (10.5.2008).
15 cf. O'Keefe, John, Nadel Lynn, The Hippocampus as a Cognitive Map, Oxford University Press, 1978; free pdf-version available, http://www.cognitivemap.net/ (10.5.2008).
16 Human Performance In: The Mental Rotation of Map Displays, 1992, Vol. 5, No. 4, Pages 303-328.
17 Arhippainen, Leena, Rantakokko, Tapani, Tähti, Marika, Navigation with an Adaptive Mobile Map-Application: User Experiences of Gesture- and Context-Sensitiveness. Ubiquitous Computing Systems, Second International Sym posium, UCS 2004, Tokyo, Japan, November 8-9, 2004, Revised Selected Papers. Springer.
18 cf. Kurzweil Ray, The Singularity Is Near, New York: Penguin, 2005.
19 cf. http://brainmeta.com (10.5.2008)
20 How believing can be seeing: study shows how context dictates what we believe we see, http://www.ucl.ac.uk/news/news-articles/0802/08021802 (10.5.2008).
21 Garling, T., Book, A., Lindberg, E., & Nilsson, T., Memory for the spatial layout of the everyday physical environment: Factors affecting rate of acquisition. Journal of Environmental Psychology, 1, 1981, 263-277.
22 Koh, Garnett et. al, Use of Virtual Environments for Acquiring Configurational Knowledge about Specific Real-World Spaces, Volume 8, Issue 6, 1999, pp. 632-656.
23 cf. Dewey, John. Democracy and Education: An Introduc-

tion to the Philosophy of Education. New York: The Free Press, 1966.

24 Bakhtin, M., Speech Genres and Other Late Essays, Translated by Vern W. McGee. Edited by Caryl Emerson and Michael Holquist, University of Texas Press: Slavic Series no. 8, 1986.

25 Corning, P., Synergy, Cybernetics, and the Evolution of Politics, 1996; http://www.complexsystems.org/publica tions/scep.html (10.5.2008).

5

1 Bolz, Norbert (2006): bang design – design manifesto of the 21st century. Hamburg: Trendbüro.

2 Interview with Otto E. Rössler (in German): Vom Chaos, der Virtuellen Realität und der Endophysik. http://www.heise.de/tp/r4/artikel/5/5004/1.html (15.11.2006).

3 Stocker, G./ Schöpf, C. (ed.) 2001: Ars Electronica 2001. Wien, New York: Springer.

4 Ghosh, R. A.: "In an environment where it costs next to nothing to duplicate a product, exactly what is scarce? A Fer rari F40 would presumably be cheaper if it cost under a dollar to make a perfect copy." http://www.firstmonday.org/is sues/issue3_3/ghosh/ (08.12.2006).

5 Kittler, F.: „Wissenschaft als Open-Source-Prozeß", http://www.mikro.org/Events/OS/ref-texte/kittler.html (08.12.2006).

6 Walser, R: "Elements of a Cyberspace Playhouse" (1990), cited in Howard Rheingold, Virtual Reality (NY: Simon & Schuster, 1992), p. 192.

7 See also Herring, S. C., Scheidt, L. A., Wright, E., and Bonus, S. (2005) Weblogs as a Bridging Genre. Information, Technology, & People, 18 (22), pp. 142-171, http://www.research.philips.com/technologies/misc/homelab/downloads/homelab_365.pdf (10.5.2008).

8 Rushkoff: 1999, p. 269.

9 cf. Gleick's "Butterfly Effect". In: Gleick, J., (1987). Chaos: The Making of a New Science. New York, NY, Penguin Books.

10 Barabási, A. L., (2002): p. 106.

11 c.f. Peter Galison, In: Latour, B. P. Weibel (2002): Iconoclash: Beyond the Image Wars in Science, Religion and Art. p. 300, ZKM & MIT Press.

12 "Complexity" was an exciting new interdisciplinary area of inquiry that emerged in the 1980's (cf. M. Mitchell Waldrop, Complexity, Touchstone, 1992), in large part because computers made it possible for the first time to make observations on the behavior of "iterative" systems.

13 Knowledge Building terminology stems from Scardamella & Bereiter, Ontario Institute for Studies in Education.

14 Refashion or Remediation (cf. Bolter/Grusin, 2000) suggests media swapping and media transfers from "old" into "new" media, the virtual into the real and vice versa, e.g. 3-D prints of Second-Life avatars (see presentation).

15 cf. M.,Okabe, D. & Matsuda, M., (2005): Personal, Port able, Pedestrian. Mobile Phones in Japanese Life. Cambridge, MA: The MIT Press.

16 http://www.friendster.com/ (10.5. 2008).

17 cf. Deleuze & Guattari in A Thousand Plateaus: Capitalism and Schizophrenia. University of Minnesota Press, 1987.

Image Sources

Gesellschaft und Wirtschaft, Bildstatistisches Elementarwerk. Leipzig 1930, p. 29.
Otto Neurath: Gesammelte bildpädagogische Schriften (Schriften Band 3, herausgegeben von Rudolf Haller und Robin Kinross), Wien: Hölder-Pichler-Tempsky 1991; p. 32.
Buckminster Fuller Institute Los Angeles, p. 49.
Archive Sonvilla-Weiss, p. 55, 80.
Lau & Vande Moere: Model of Information Aesthetics. p. 63.
"Sound/Chair" by Matthew Plummer Fernandez, "Sounds of "Complexity by Mattia Casalegno, Enzo Varriale. p. 70.
Screenshot, http://www.well-formed-data.net/experiments/lifestream_mashup/ p. 76.
Eva and Franco Mattes aka 0100101110101101.ORG, Reenactment of Joseph Beuys' 7000 Oaks Synthetic Performance in Second Life, 2007. Courtesy Postmasters gallery, New York. p. 85.
Jeremy Bentham, Plan of the Panopticon. The works of Jeremy Bentham vol. IV, 172-3, 1843. p. 88.
The Internet Encyclopedia of Science, cloaking device. p. 99.
Image capture from Flash animation, http://news.mc.duke.edu/filebank/2003/10/41/Robot_arm.swf, p. 107.
Scott Snibbe, Boundary Functions, 1998. http://snibbe.com/scott/bf/, p. 116.
Benedict Radcliffe, Wire frame sculpture, p.155. Public photo: http://www.flickr.com/photos/benterrett/382144700/in/photostream/

Bibliography

Anderson, C. (2006), The Long Tail: Why the Future of Business is Selling Less of More. New York: Hyperion.

Barabási, A.-L. (2003), Linked: How Everything Is Connect ed to Everything Else and What It Means for Business, Science, and Everyday Life. NY: Plume Books.

Baudrillard, J. (1996), Simulacra and Simulation. Michigan: University of Michigan Press.

Baudrillard, J. (2005), The Conspiracy of Art: Manifestos, Interviews. Edited by Sylvere Lotringer and Translated by Ames Hodges. New York: Semiotext(e).

Bauman Z. (1998), Globalization – The Human Conequences. Cambridge: Polity.

Beck, U. (1986), Risikogesellschaft. Auf dem Weg in eine an dere Moderne. Frankfurt a/M: Suhrkamp.

Bereiter, C. (2002), Education and Mind in the Knowledge Age. Mahwah, NY: Lawrence Erlbaum Associates.

Bolter, D., Grusin, R. (2000), Remediation: Understanding New Media. Cambridge, MA: MIT Press.

Bolz, N. (2006), bang design. design manifest des 21. Jahrhunderts. Hamburg: Trend Büro.

Carr, N. (2008), The Big Switch: Rewiring the World, from Edison to Google. New York: Norton.

Carbone, M. (2004), The Thinking of the Sensible: Merleau-Ponty's A-Philosophy, Evanston: Northwestern University Press.

Certeau de, M. (1984), The Practice of Everyday Life. Los An geles: University of California Press.

Deleuze, G., Guattari, F. (1994), A Thousand Plateaus: Capitalism and Schizophrenia. Minnesota: University of

Minnesota Press.
Dewey, J. (1966), Democracy and education: An introduction to the philosophy of education. New York: Free Press.
Fidler, R. (1997), Mediamorphosis: Understanding New Media. Thousand Oaks, CA: Pine Forge Press.
Foucault, M. (1978), Discipline & Punish: The Birth of the Prison. New York: Random House.
Freire, P. (1985), The politics of education: Culture power and liberation. (D. Macedo, Trans.) Westport: Bergin and Garvey.
Freire, P. (1993), Pedagogy of the Oppressed. Revised ed. (M. Bergman Ramos, Trans.) New York: Continuum.
Fry, B. (2004), Computational Information Design. MIT Boston: Dissertation.
Galison, P. In: Latour, B., Weibel, p. (2002), Iconoclash: Beyond the Image Wars in Science, Religion and Art. Cambridge, MA: MIT Press.
Garfinkel, H. (1967), Studies in ethnomethodology. New York: Englewood Cliffs.
Geisler C. et al. (2001), Border Crossings: The Social Transformation of the Boundary between Work and Life by It Gone Mobile [On-line White Paper], Rensselaer Polytechnic Institute.
Gelernter, D. (1992), Mirror Worlds: or the Day Software Puts the Universe in a Shoebox...How It Will Happen and What It Will Mean. New York: Oxford University Press.
Gershenfeld, N. (2000), When Things Start to Think. New York: Henry Holt.
Gleick, J. (1987), Chaos: The Making of a New Science. New York: Penguin Books.
Hall, E. (1966), The Hidden Dimension. N.Y.: Doubleday.
Herring, S. C.; Scheidt, L. A.; Wright, E.; and Bonus, S.

(2005), Weblogs as a Bridging Genre: Information, Technology, & People, 18 (22), pp. 142–171.

Jenkins, H. (2006), Convergence Culture: Where Old and New Media Collide. New York: New York University Press.

Kittler, F. (1997), Literature, Media, Information Systems (Critical Voices in Art, Theory and Culture). Amsterdam: OPA.

Kurzweil, R. (2005), The Singularity Is Near: When Humans Transcend Biology. New York: Penguin.

Lacan, J. (1998), The Four Fundamental Concepts of Psychoanalysis (The Seminar of Jacques Lacan , Book 11).

Lakoff, G. (1995), Body, brain and communication. In J. Brook & I. Boal (Eds.), Resisting the virtual life. San Francisco: City Lights.

Levy, P. (1998), Becoming Virtual: Reality in the Digital Age. New York: Plenum Trade.

Maar, C.; Burda H. (2004), Iconic Turn. Die neue Macht der Bilder. Köln: Dumont.

Manovich, L., Kratky, A. (2005) Soft Cinema: Navigating the Database. Cambridge, MA: MIT Press.

Merleau-Ponty, M. (1958), Phenomenology of Perception. London: Routledge.

Mitchell W.J.T. (1986), Iconology. Image, Text, Ideology. Chicago: The University of Chicago Press.

Norman, D. (1998), The Invisible Computer. Cambridge, MA: MIT Press.

Otlet, P. (1934), Documentation Le Livre Sur Le Livre. Théorie et Pratique. Bruxelles: Van Keerberghen & fils.

Rayward B. (1975), The Universe of Information. The work of Paul Otlet for documentation and international organisation. Moscow: All-Union Institute for Scientific and Technical Information (VINITI).

Rushkoff, D. (1999), Playing the Future: What We Can Learn from Digital Kids. New York: Riverhead Books.

Sonvilla-Weiss, S. (2005), (e)Pedagogy – Visual Knowledge Building. Bern: Peter Lang.

Sonvilla-Weiss, S. (2008), Art, Science and Education. In: Alexenberg, M. (2008), Educating Artists for the Future: Learning at the Intersections of Art, Science, Technology and Culture. Chicago: University of Chicago Press.

Stephenson, N. (1992), Snow Crash. New York: Bentham.

Stocker, G./ Schöpf, C. (eds.) (2001), Ars Electronica 2001. Wien, New York: Springer.

Stocker, G./ Schöpf, C. (eds.) (2003), Code - The Language of Our Time, Ars Electronica 2003. Osterfildern-Ruit: Hatje Cantz.

Žižek, S. (2003). Organs Without Bodies. London: Routledge.

Žižek, S. (1989). The Sublime Object of Ideology. London: Verso.

Tapscott, D., Ticoll, D. (2003), The Naked Corporation: How the Age of Transparency Will Revolutionize Business.

Tapscott, D., Williams, A. (2008), Wikinomics: How Mass Collaboration Changes Everything. New York: Penguin.

Tufte, E. (1990), Envisioning Information. Chesire: Graphic Presss.

Tufte, E. (1997), Visual Explanations. Images and Quantities, Evidence and Narrative. Chesire: Graphic Presss.

Virilio, P. (1996), Fluchtgeschwindigkeit. München: Hanser.

Vossoughian N. (2008), Otto Neurath. The Language of the Global Polis. Rotterdam: NAi Publishers.

Walser, R. (1990), Elements of a Cyberspace Playhouse, cited in Howard Rheingold, Virtual Reality. New York: Simon &

Schuster.
Waldrop, M. (1992), Complexity: The Emerging Science at the Edge of Order and Chaos. NY: Touchstone.
Weibel, P. (2004). Gamma und Amplitude: medien- und kunsttheoretische Schriften. Berlin: Fundus.

Bei Fragen zur Produktsicherheit wenden Sie sich bitte an:
If you have any questions regarding product safety,
please contact:

Birkhäuser Verlag GmbH
Im Westfeld 8
4055 Basel, Schweiz
productsafety@degruyterbrill.com